D1256311

BLUEPRINT
FOR
A BRIGHTER
CHILD

BLUEPRINT FOR A BRIGHTER CHILD

*Brandon Sparkman
and Ann Carmichael*

McGraw-Hill Book Company

New York | St. Louis | San Francisco

Düsseldorf | London | Mexico

Sydney | Toronto

This book was set in Caledo by University Graphics, Inc.

123456789BPBP79876543

Library of Congress Cataloging in Publication Data

Sparkman, Brandon.
  Blueprint for a brighter child.

    1. Children—Management. 2. Domestic education—
United States. 3. Parent and child. I. Carmichael,
Ann, joint author. II. Title.
HQ772.S65   649'.5   72-10307
ISBN 0-07-059890-8

Dedicated to
Ricky, Rita, and Robert
Larry and Beth
who taught us much of what we know

Contents

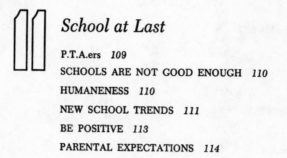

Foreword

Some years ago we participated in a unique preschool program at the Child Development Center in Tuscumbia, Alabama—a program whose distinctiveness lay not in the originality of its parts, but in the way its parts were woven together. One of the most innovative features, we felt, was the involvement of the children's parents in the venture: they were brought together bimonthly at the Center (1) to discuss general matters related to their children's welfare, (2) to watch a videotaped program of a teacher teaching a specific skill or concept to their children, (3) to discuss their children's need for learning such skills and concepts and the method adults should use in teaching them, and (4) to make a developmental game, utilizing the pattern provided by the parent coordinator, to reinforce at home the skill or concept they had observed being taught to their children. The parents were obviously enthusiastic—they had begun to realize what education was about, and they were helping their children to learn.

"Why hasn't someone shown us how to help our children learn before now?" one parent asked us. "We have wasted four years of their lives because no one cared enough to show us how to help them." Other parents echoed these words, and we realized how necessary it was to show parents how they can help their children grow—intellectually, psychologically, and physically—in the preschool years.

For a time we were separated from each other by distance and changes in employment, but we still longed to tell other parents what we had learned in Tuscumbia. Finally we made a commitment—somehow we would set aside the time to write a book as unusual as the preschool program we helped to design and implement a few years earlier. Each of us wrote certain chapters of the book alone, but always we told our story in the first person singular—we hoped it would seem as if we were talking to our readers.

We wish to express appreciation to Mrs. Virginia Clark, director of Tuscumbia's Child Development Center, for her leadership in utilizing the creative abilities of her staff, all of whom contributed many of the ideas in this book. We wish also to thank Dr. Walter Barbe for encouraging us, and for reading the manuscript and offering constructive criticism; Mildred Hust and Mayedelle McKelvey for editorial suggestions; Betsy Grimes for assisting with the illustrations; and, last but not least, Wanda Sparkman and Archie Carmichael for enduring our neglect of them while the manuscript was in preparation.

Brandon Sparkman
Ann Carmichael

The Importance of the Preschool Years

School readiness begins when a baby breathes his first breath. Some potentials and some limitations for learning are set at the moment of conception, but hereditary factors may be of less importance than people suspect. The opportunities for developing the potentials and overcoming the limitations genetically imposed are primarily limited by the knowledge and imagination of those with whom the child comes in contact during his preschool and primary school years.

There are numerous ways one can boost the learning power of children, but to do so one must introduce them to appropriate experiences and activities during the preschool years. Once the child is old enough to enroll in first grade, it is too late to greatly affect his learning potential. If you are interested in increasing the likelihood of your child's academic success, in expanding his intellectual capability and instilling in him a love for learning, you must begin while he is quite young—

in fact, the earlier you begin the more success you can expect.

The school has been given the monumental job of educating the youth of America. Yet, the degree to which this task can be accomplished is, at best, reduced by the limitations imposed upon children by the damning effects of environmental and intellectual starvation, which have been all too obvious to me in my years of experience with Headstart and with elementary-school-age children. Although many of the deprived children with whom I have worked overcame some of their imposed handicaps, other educational impediments will persist throughout life. Current research indicates that the line a child's mental development will take is determined between the tenth and the eighteenth months of life, and that basic human attitudes and the psychological learning patterns of children are pretty well established at age three. By age four a child has probably learned half of all he will ever learn. If these findings are accurate, then parents must play a unique role in the realization of their children's potential and enjoyment of learning.

This book will deal in some measure with child growth and development as it relates to the educational process, but more importantly it will describe activities of a simple and pleasurable nature which you can use in preparing your child for school. Learning should be fun both at home and at school. Therefore, each game and each learning endeavor included is meant to be introduced as a natural, happy, parent-child routine, not as part of the formalized teaching-learning situation characterized by so many of the primary schools of our nation.

In order to examine the purposes of education — not in the educational jargon so common to many of us, but in simple, easy-to-understand, realistic terms — perhaps it would be desirable at this point to focus briefly on the school. Since our knowledge is increasing rapidly, we know that we cannot acquire and retain complete information on all subjects — education must be more than a storing of information. What, then, is the practical route to take in educating our children? How about the development of a positive self-perception and of self-responsibility within the individual? To this you might add the acquisition of basic reading and math skills, and a lot of love for learning, and you would be well on the way. "But how is this done?" you ask. My answer is that it begins with you and your child as soon as he—or she—is born.

There are many enjoyable and satisfying activities you can plan, and certain ways in which you can behave, each of which will have a tremendous impact upon shaping the attitudes of your child, particularly in relation to "love of learning." When you have helped your child to observe the world about him and to organize his perceptions into meaningful concepts, he has acquired the basis for further intellectual development. If the learning experiences are arranged in such ways that they are enjoyable to both child and parent, pleasure becomes associated with learning and tends to develop in the child initiative for further learning. When learning is exciting it becomes its own reward, and the child begins to accept the responsibility for further inquiry. That is what education is about—helping children develop a love for learning, teaching them about sources of information and procedures for acquiring it —then shifting the responsibility for learning to the learner. Formal schooling does not go on forever. What happens to the youngster who leaves school without these tools?

MENTAL NOURISHMENT

Some psychologists say that a child is like a flower— if he is left alone he will blossom in due time. But I wish to point out that proper water and nourishment, along with regular cultivation and protection from disease, will insure a more lovely flower. Time is important, but time alone will not bring about a happy, adjusted, well-rounded, contributing adult. Love is needed, too, but passive love is not enough. A child must have competent, loving individuals who demonstrate their love by guiding him through numerous and appropriate learning experiences.

But you ask, "How do I help my child develop this love for learning—this initiative and self-responsibility?" That's what the following chapters are about. All children need attention and most parents are willing, and even eager, to satisfy this need. Through becoming aware of developmental learning activities parents can turn much of the parent-child playtime into valuable learning experiences with no curtailment of pleasure. The time to begin is now. If your child has not yet arrived, begin planning for the arrival. Think in terms of creating a stimulating physical environment for him. After this is accomplished, turn your thoughts toward scheduling your time so that adequate attention can be given the youngster. Then work out, pretty much in detail, games and activities appropriate for each stage of development—games and activities which fit as naturally as possible into daily routines. If you already have a preschooler, begin where he is. It isn't difficult. It only takes a little know-how for parents such as you—those who love and enjoy their children, those willing to devote a small amount of time to "child's play"—to set the stage for a lifetime of adventures in learning.

CHAPTER 2

Begin at the Beginning

So often a beginning is over before we realize anything has actually happened. When did a particular friendship begin, or the sun set, or summer commence? Infancy is short lived—so short, in fact, that it is important to see it as a prescribed period of time. I am not suggesting that you would not recognize a beginning with a new baby, but parents every day are "beginning" with a new child without being aware of the importance of those first months.

Many young mothers purchase books to discover what all new mothers need to know, such as when should the baby eat, take naps, and be taken for checkups; but mothers need other kinds of direction also. It has been my experience, and that of many of my professional friends, that there is a definite lack of information about an infant's early needs, particularly about those relating to his cognitive or academic growth.

Understanding the importance of the beginning may seem a superficial concept, but grasping its full implications can shape your behavior—assuring you of enabling your child to develop his greatest potential. Just as the initial strokes of a painting set the result of a picture, your initial contact with an infant sets his future development. The beginning to which I refer consists of all the experiences your baby has in those first months of life: the initial perception of sound, light, touch, movement, and his relationship with you. As you anticipate these joy-filled times, you should carefully consider the baby's surroundings.

DOORS TO LEARNING

The senses are the doors to your baby's mind. All the information he receives will come through the doors of the five senses: seeing, hearing, tasting, touching, and smelling. When you plan your baby's surroundings you will want them, and your association with the baby, to give these senses an opportunity to operate. See that there are many things to see, hear, touch, taste, and smell. Early stimulation of the senses makes your baby more aware of his surroundings; and as he reacts to each new stimulus he will be able to perceive even more and to make finer distinctions in the particulars of his expanding world. This early stimulation and reaction will establish a pattern for learning which will be crucial to his later learning experience.

OBJECTS FOR SIGHT STIMULATION

As a new baby spends much of his time in his crib, he should have interesting objects to see, and things to touch and hear. Mobiles can be purchased to suspend from the crib railings. The only caution is to be sure that the things that can be reached are safe for handling and mouthing, because initially everything a baby touches goes into his mouth. This is a normal first stage of development, and being aware of the purpose it serves will enable you to plan accordingly. Not only are handling and tasting sources of pleasure to the infant, they are also learning experiences. The sucking activity is largely satisfied through feeding; but because it is pleasurable, the infant will also attempt to put everything else in his mouth. Through such experiences he learns characteristics of objects.

You might enjoy making mobiles yourself. If you use your imagination, your product could more nearly fit the learning experiences you plan for your child than ready-made items would. Because the homemade product is inexpensive, you could change the mobiles every few days. This is an improvement in itself. My first child looked at the same six bright plastic birds hanging on strings for twelve months. You can improve upon that. Your baby's ability to touch objects will come a little later, so perhaps your first selection might be bright paper shapes. Straws are wonderful to work with because they can be cut to fit in many different ways. Pipe cleaners are pliable. By using various combinations of articles, you can create very attractive mobiles.

OBJECTS FOR AUDIO STIMULATION

A variation on the mobile might be patterned after the wind chime. Household objects such as cookie cutters, which would tinkle from a slight breeze, could be great fun for the baby. The basic hardware of the purchased mobiles would be helpful in making this kind of mobile, but others could be hung from a coat hanger or from the ceiling to provide yet another change. One additional feature of mobiles is the opportunity they afford the baby to observe a simple cause-effect relationship. You may shake the bed, and the objects move. Later the baby shakes the bed, or inadvertently makes some motion that moves the mobile. The light dawns: shaking the bed makes the objects move, just as crying brings food or dry diapers. Learning is taking place. The same kinds of responses can come from the com-

mercially prepared bed toys that string across the crib with a rattle, a bell, or a pull-type grasping rod: as the baby discovers his arm and accidentally brushes the object, he elicits sounds from it. Soon he will make this a purposeful action. Just as he moved the bed to shake the mobile, he exercises his arm to hear the bell.

BEYOND THE CRIB

After a few weeks your baby's perception will extend beyond the crib to the room itself. Perception happens only when there are things to perceive, and if you use bright colors imaginatively—in pictures, murals, or commercial cutouts—you will encourage your child's perceptual development.

The use of crib bumpers has been criticized because the child who sleeps on his stomach will probably be completely screened from his surroundings in this prone position. Transparent vinyl bumpers are available that will remedy this disadvantage, or you can place the baby on his back part of the time. Lying on the stomach, however, is crucial to muscle strengthening, development, and, according to a certain theory, neurological patterning. Given opportunities, most babies will engage in physical and visual activities automatically as they mature.

Another aspect of the baby's surroundings that should be considered is that of listening experiences. Many baby beds have musical attachments that play a single tune. Much better than this attachment is a small record player and a selection of appropriate records. These could be infinitely more pleasing in the variety they afford. Providing music is one way to stimulate a child's perception of sounds. Because the sense of hearing is one of the two most important senses in acquiring information and future learning, it is worthy of your attention even at this early age. An extra dividend might be the establishment of a routine that would make turning out the light an enjoyable experience—you could provide pleasant music by which to end the day, and you would be helping your baby toward a subconscious appreciation of good music. The most important sounds that your baby will hear, however, will come from you.

Now we come to the most crucial aspects of your baby's surroundings—you. Don't be offended by the thought that you are just part of the surroundings. In the early days of his life, your baby doesn't even distinguish between himself and his environment. He doesn't know where he stops and you begin. While your child is in this completely vulnerable and dependent early state, you are literally the source of life and comfort for him. You provide food and care, meeting the basic needs vital to life. You relieve the tension of hunger, and discomforts of various kinds. You hold him gently and speak lovingly. At this point, you are the baby's first experience in a relationship, and for a long while it's a very one-sided kind of relationship. Many books have been written on this subject alone: the importance of the mother-child relationship, and the effects of this first attachment on the child's later perception of himself and his relationship to others. They all underscore the fact that not only your child's social and emotional health but also his intellectual growth depends on the quality of his relationship with his parents. Infants reared in institutional settings have been known to become apathetic and withdrawn—they are often considered mentally retarded. Later comparisons showed that infants who had been handled, cared for, and played with by mentally retarded women in the same institution had achieved much more normal development.

More recent research conducted by the Harvard Pre-School Project not only substantiates the earlier findings, but adds new dimensions. This study designates the age of ten to eighteen months as the period when the mental development of a child is determined, and it identifies experiences and relationships which are critical to maximum development.

It appears that one-year-olds, left to themselves, spent one-fifth of their waking hours staring intently at objects as if memorizing their features. Another large portion of their time is spent in experimentation, testing their physical prowess, determining how things work and why, and developing interpersonal relationships.

As they grow older, certain of these children do exceptionally well in almost all aspects of living. They solve daily problems, do well in school academically, get along well on the playground, and relate well to other individuals. Others almost never seem able to cope with the existing situation. What makes the difference?

The child who does well has a mother who (1) provides a rich variety of objects and toys for play, (2) allows freedom to roam and discover, (3) gives attention to her child when he finds something unusually exciting or when he encounters a problem which he cannot overcome, (4) turns everyday situations into games, and (5) talks to her child.

Mothers of children who later demonstrate ineptness are much more protective. They usually restrict their children's environments by placing them in cribs, playpens, or highchairs much of the time. They restrict areas where their children may roam. "No, no" is heard often in their houses, and there is a scarcity of play objects for their children. The mothers are not readily available to their children; they talk less to them; they fail to share their babies' excitement and seldom give them mental stimulation.

The amount of time you devote to your child is not nearly so important as how the available time is spent and the fact that some time is available. Short ten- to twenty-second interludes, in which you offer a word of advice, a new idea, or a different way of looking at things, will increase your child's curiosity and stimulate his mental processes.

One of the most important skills a child can develop is that of using adults as a resource. Children who generally function at a high level know how to gain the attention and help of those around them; during your own child's early years you are that source of help.

You are able and eager to love and care for your little one because it brings joy, and possibly a long-awaited fulfillment, to you. You must consider the far-reaching repercussions of the simple acts you perform in these first months. You must realize that nothing could be more important than what you do with your own time and how you do it. It is possible to let time slip by unnoticed in the routine of a schedule, but you can provide extra dividends for your child by not becoming enslaved by routine. Of course an infant needs the security and regularity of a schedule, but he needs you to be more than perfunctory in your care of him. Feeding times seem to come regularly, but in the perspective of a lifetime they are over rather quickly. A relaxed, warm, loving setting for feeding is a must—if you are too busy to hold a bottle, you are too busy with unimportant things. When you are through feeding, you can encourage the baby's responsiveness by taking an extra five minutes to cuddle him, play with him, repeat his sounds, call him by name, guide physical motions with his hands and legs. When a new baby arrives, you may be so anxious to deal with any jealousy in an older child, and to make him feel secure, that it is easy to allow a good little baby to just be good all by himself. He will lie in his bed for hours without crying—so you let him, in order to attend to the older child's needs. The solution is to budget time in advance. Consider your responsibilities, your best working and resting pace, and make a schedule allowing time for your baby's and toddler's needs as well as for your household responsibilities. This does not mean living by a prefixed timetable, not at all; by anticipating what you want to accomplish and how much time you have to do it in, you can make sure that you include all the things you need to include. If you work full time or even part time, you should arrange your schedule so that a goodly portion of your "at home" time can be spent with your child. Furthermore, you should exercise great care in the selection of a mother or father substitute for your away-from-home hours. Anyone entrusted with the continuing care of a young child should talk to him and play with him occasionally just as you might do.

AWARENESS OF DEVELOPMENTAL STAGES

If you are not already familiar with the basic stages of child development or with children's normal growth patterns, it will add much to your interest in and pleasure with your child to acquire this information: one father commented that watching his child had become fun in a new way—like watching a football game having well-executed plays. Several good books are available on this subject. I do not intend to make you feel pressure, or to make you feel you must put pressure upon your child to move from one stage to another. These are maturational stages and should be considered only as observation points. All children *are* different— beautifully so, unique. Yet within a range of variation there are common landmarks children pass that you can observe. Knowledge of these maturational stages, besides helping you "zero in" on the child, so to speak, will also guide you in designing appropriate activities and in interpreting behavior. For instance, when your baby became six months old he was able to grasp and mouth his rattle, even shake it. But now he is reaching the stage in which he can let go of it. This maturational stage has just appeared. He drops his rattle, looks over the side of the crib or highchair; you pick it up; he immediately drops it again—just because he can! "How interesting! It's not part of me—I can drop it." Of course, these are not conscious thoughts, but the beginning of awareness, and if you know the baby is not being

12

naughty, you will cooperate. Then you share in a learning moment by playing this game of drop and retrieve only to drop again. When you do not have time to play, with this knowledge you won't be annoyed by the baby's actions. You also will have the clue that your child is ready to have some objects to handle—large enough, but not too large.

TOYS FOR THE VERY YOUNG

Gross or large muscle development comes before finer muscle control, and the early motions will be quite lacking in refinement. Highchair toys which attach to the tray by suction offer a variety of action responses for your baby after he is able to use his hands and arms. Sponge blocks, cool silver rattles or spoons, rubber squeeze toys, clear plastic toys, some filled with bright objects floating in fluid, are all objects that can be handled with satisfaction and safety. Toy manufacturers are becoming increasingly aware of the potential hazards of some play objects, but naturally the responsibility ultimately rests with you to exercise judgment. Teddy bears with removable eyes, squeeze toys with a noisemaker that works out when squeezed, and other such toys are, of course, things to avoid.

BODY AWARENESS

At some point accompanying the initial handling of appropriate toys and objects, the baby begins to develop an awareness of himself and his own body. When he drops his rattle, he is learning, "I am not the rattle." A universal and very entertaining sight is the baby who has just discovered his own toes. He "sees" them, he reaches for them, pulls them, puts them in his mouth. To him they are completely entertaining and absorbing. It will be some time before he will move on to other body discoveries, but this is the beginning. You can spend some profitable moments playing a "body game" when the baby is about six months old. Say "This is the baby's arm" and move the arm in a playful fashion; "This is [using your baby's name] leg," bend up his leg; "This is baby's hand," bend it back and forth; "This is baby's finger," move it back and forth; "This is baby's nose," tap it lightly; "This is baby's ear," pull his ear lobe. You are not trying to teach words at this stage, but you are affording the baby his fun and aiding in his development of body awareness.

An increasing awareness of himself also increases his awareness of his surroundings. In other words, if the baby knows where he is, he also knows where he is not. When a baby is between six and eight months old, his interest in his surroundings greatly expands. His curiosity increases rapidly, and at the same time his physical maturation reaches a point where he can crawl around to investigate his changing world. He can pull up to look it over; and, of course, he will put as much of it as possible into his mouth. Your reaction to these developments is important and requires patience and insight on your part.

EARLY EXPLORATION

As your crawler begins moving around, his developing relationship with his world becomes analogous to his initial relationship with you. How he experiences and accomplishes this relationship will set future expectations and patterns of responses, just as his initial experiences with you predispose his future relationships with other people. Size up your house and establish several places where your child is free to explore and move about without restrictions. You may be intent upon leaving in place such objects as the good ashtrays, and upon teaching your child what "no" means; and of course this does have its place, but so does freedom for discovery—a big place! Your child's future learning experiences depend upon his curiosity and initiative— the innate drive to discover and to understand his world. The first experiences should be encouraged within the

14

bounds of reason and safety. Choose a place where things cannot be pulled down or tipped over, but leave enough to provide interesting experiences. When my oldest child was a baby, I remember emptying a bottom drawer of a cabinet in the kitchen and putting some pans, utensils, plastic objects and toys within easy reach of the youngster as an attractive alternative to the inevitable "no-no."

If you use a playpen for part of the day while you are doing housework, put in a variety of toys and interesting material. Move it to different places, if possible, to change the scenery. Budget some time for your baby's crawling—and, later, toddling—to discover things inside and outside of the house.

It is well to remember the importance of communication even at this early age. Talk to your baby. Your sounds may not be understood as far as the words themselves are concerned, but the tone of your voice and the comforting experience of your attempts to communicate will be important.

THE ABSORBENT MIND

Maria Montessori, a renowned pioneer in early childhood education, observed that a child is in the period of "the absorbent mind" from the ages of two and a half to three. During this time the young child learns at a rate never again equaled—"soaking up" information indiscriminately through every experience. What he learns is what he is exposed to directly; a stimulating environment is a must for the infant and early toddler. Later, between the ages of approximately three and six, the mind becomes more selective, and Montessori refers to this time span as a child's "sensitive period." There will be a particular time when the mind is sensitive to a specific area of skill, and learning can take place at an accelerated rate. Yet the emphasis is still on absorption. Of course there has to be action, and interaction, with concrete objects for this learning to take place.

15

Montessori's observations, made in the early 1900s, correspond with the more recent research of another childhood education expert, Jean Piaget, who refers to the child up to age eighteen months as in the "sensori-motor period"—physically maturing and experiencing the world through each sense. From eighteen months to seven years of age, Piaget speaks of the child as being in the "pre-operational period"—the child is developing language skills very rapidly, and absorbing information, filing away bits of experiences, and picking up or learning the attributes of a multitude of objects as he acts on his environment. The third stage in the child's preschool classification is the "operational period" when he begins to think logically, drawing upon the information he has gathered and made his own. Piaget's theory of how children learn—by assimilation and accommodation—has tremendously expanded understanding in the area of development of intelligence in children.

Both authorities, Montessori and Piaget, observed children's behavior in an effort to understand their learning patterns and to use this increased understanding to plan children's learning experiences more effectively. Montessori and Piaget also demonstrated the child's early curiosity, and his almost limitless capacity for absorbing information at a very early age. Each also saw that the child's later learning experiences were directly dependent upon his having had the opportunity to use this early potential. It *is* important to begin at the beginning.

CHAPTER 3

Learning to See

One is often startled by the discovery of a building which he has never seen. A scene of rare beauty in the surrounding landscape is often taken in with delight only after its existence has been pointed out by another. Many unusually interesting and lovely things are never seen by those of us who peruse the world about us with limited observational techniques. Lack of training places some limitations on our ability to see things in general, and when it comes to observing details, one almost always sees only what he is trained to see. He is incapable of seeing minute differences without having them specifically pointed out to him.

A few years ago I was called upon to establish a printing shop in the local school system where I worked. Having had no previous experience in printing, and primarily out of curiosity, I decided to train alongside the inexperienced printer we had employed. In the training process I learned to look for flaws in printing, and, to my amazement, they were so numerous in newspapers that they were very distracting until I got over my printing "kick." But the point is that I had never seen them until I was trained to see them—and the same thing is true of the world about us. We see so little of the earth's beauty because we have never been trained to see the arrays, arrangements, patterns, and activities which are all around us.

A WALK AROUND THE BLOCK

Let's take a walk around the average block. Not by the seashore nor through the wooded area nearby, but just around any ordinary residential block.

While we walk slowly along, our child skips and runs and jumps and comes back to greet us with an occasional superficial observation—which presents a wonderful opportunity for enlarged observation. We might stop on the grassy strip by the sidewalk and stoop to examine the blades of grass. Look at the different kinds of grass—the shape of the blades, the color, and the veins running through each blade. Pull up a sprig and note the roots. A few leaves could be taken home to study, arrange, or mount, and a collection is begun. Questions about the way plants eat and drink might be in order. Through simple yet provoking questions a child's curiosity can be aroused; very simple explanations can satisfy curious minds, but extensive and high-level explanations can easily discourage questions.

Hours could easily be spent here looking for animals living in the grass. The animal that probably has already come to your mind is the ant. These interesting creatures could absorb much time and open the way for continued excitement. This would be an excellent time to find pictures of ants in books—especially in children's encyclopedias. What a good way to get a child further interested in books! Now would be a good time to read to him about ants, ant houses, grass, and leaves. You might be interested in buying a glass ant house or in making one of your own by filling a gallon glass jar to within three inches of the top with dirt and ants from one particular ant hill. Be careful that no alien ants are accidentally included in the new habitat, or war will break out and all the ants will be destroyed. A small amount of sugar dissolved in water and sprinkled on the soil in the jar will provide food for the ants. Water must be added regularly to provide moisture for the environment. After a few days tunnels will appear along the sides of the jar and much of the activity inside will be visible.

But back to the wilds of the block. What other animals can you find? Do you see a dog or cat? If so, are these animals too? How are animals different? How are they alike? Are we animals?

Did you notice the soil around the ant hill? Is it different from the soil in other places around the block? And how is soil made? Speaking of soil—is soil good or bad? We clean our feet before going inside the house so we won't track soil inside. Does this mean that soil is bad? Is soil like most other things—good or bad depending upon its location and use?

Flowers in bloom are a perfect choice to help your child develop the concept of color. Don't strive to make him memorize the colors around him; merely make him aware of the different colors. By simply referring to the green grass, the red flower, the black pavement, you will promote color consciousness and color discrimination. Children love games and a good one in this instance is the old-timer, "I see something red. What do I see?" Of course, taking turns is a must.

Look at those trees—see the ways they are alike and the ways they are different? Even the same species are different, yet all have likenesses. There may be a cocoon on one of them—or a bird's nest—or holes where birds have pecked for insects—or knots—or dead limbs. The bark is somewhat like our skin. Notice the overall shape of the leaves. Are they round—triangular—pointed? Look at the symmetry of the edges—and, by the way, these leaves have veins like those in grass blades—which means that leaves and grass are alike.

As for those flowers we observed along the way—look at the petals, pollen, pistil and other plant paraphernalia later. We don't want to overdo it on this trip. We haven't even looked at the houses yet—the big houses—bigger houses—biggest house. Which house is smallest? These are important concepts—concepts essential to academic success in grade one. But back to nature.

Are there clouds in the sky? What do they look like? Can you see faces, animals, buildings, or other figures in the clouds? How would they feel if you could touch them? (This question might be answered some foggy morning.) What can clouds tell you? Curiosity aroused at this time might be spurred on by further cloud-watching on days when it is obviously going to rain. Even a walk in the rain under an umbrella could be exciting. Hear the raindrops? How does rain feel? Is it hot or cold? Is rain good or bad? Where does rain go? Does the grass drink it? Rainy days are good days for story telling, especially stories like "Noah's Ark." Be sure to include the rainbow part, about God's promise!

As we walk along we can't see the wind but we can see what the wind does. It blows the leaves and our hair and it feels cool. But sometime it feels hot. Where does the wind come from? You can't answer all the questions, but that's good. There are other sources of information, and your child should be made aware of this fact. Today leaves are blowing toward the east. Yesterday they were blowing south. What does south mean?

For some reason most children get excited about rocks. In most neighborhoods you can find rocks of many different colors, sizes, shapes, hardnesses, and compositions. Rocks are a wonderful source for a collection. Help your child see rocks, feel them—yes, even throw them. See what happens when a rock goes up—when it comes down—when it hits the pavement or ground at an angle—how it sounds—which kinds of rocks break—which kinds do not break. Count rocks—read about them—look at pictures of rocks—enjoy their beauty.

We could spend a week on one trip, but a child cannot benefit from a prolonged examination of all facets of nature, so don't overdo it. After all, the block will be here for a long time—so remember to point out how things change. The grass gets bigger, dies. The leaves are small, then larger; yellow, then brown. They fall to the ground and decay. New leaves replace them in the spring.

We have only been around the block. We didn't talk about the sun, moon, stars, or birds, or about a multitude of other observable objects and creatures. An extensive study could be made of birds—your imagination could take you on and on. And speaking of imagination, help your child develop a vivid one. Let him describe what he "sees" when you are reading something appropriate to such an activity. The ability to form a mental image is vital to school success and it grows out of experiences with real objects.

If so much can be seen in one block, imagine what marvelous experiences parent and child can have at the zoo, seashore, forest, lake, or wherever they might be. Any place is a place for learning, and if your child has developed a vivid imagination, games and activities can be devised from the most ordinary objects or situations. Observations and activities such as those first described lead to school readiness.

Readiness for school is based primarily upon the ability of a child to see—that is, to discriminate between colors, sizes, or even the numerals 2 and 4. Teach your child to see—to be curious—to see beauty—to enjoy living and learning. This love of learning will pay dividends. Seasons change, life goes on, and a child is helped to discover their fullest meaning and enjoyment.

CHAPTER

Language Is the Key

The brains of rats from a stimulating environment have a heavier, thicker cortex, a better blood supply, larger brain cells, more glia cells, and increased activity of brain enzymes than those of rats from deprived environments. Dr. David Krech, Professor of Psychology, University of California, and his co-workers conducted research in which one group of rats was placed in an "intellectually enriched" environment—one in which they were free to roam around in a large, object-filled space—and another group was placed in a "deprived environment." After eighty days of differential treatment the animals' brains were dissected and tested, and the results were astounding: learning experiences had actually brought about physical as well as behavioral changes in the rats. Perhaps you are not interested in rat psychology—neither am I, but for the sake of humanity this research must not go unnoticed, for it may be one of the most significant studies of the present generation.

What are the experiences which children need to bring about the greatest development of the human brain? Dr. Krech believes that language is the key.

Man is the only animal that has developed an intelligent language system. Only man is capable of talking intelligently, of reading, writing, and reasoning. In addition, he can listen with understanding while his fellow man speaks in symbols. The exercise of this unique quality surely tends to add to the capacity for further mental development. One can easily note the rapid progress young children make in speech development once they master a few words. On the other hand, limitations in understanding are evident among those with limited vocabularies. For example, a person is almost totally inept at thinking in terms of mathematics until he has mastered some mathematical vocabulary. After mastery, and only then, can he develop in the field of mathematics.

The ability to think is dependent upon language development because thinking is achieved in terms of language. As new words and new concepts are added to a child's experiential background, he gains increased capacity for thinking. As the mental processes involved in thinking operate, the processes are couched in verbal expression. To an extremely high degree, academic success in school depends upon language development.

IS YOUR CHILD DEPRIVED?

Recent research has shown that the scores deprived children make on intelligence tests can be substantially improved through concentrated efforts on language development. My own experience with deprived preschoolers has revealed that an increase of fifteen to twenty I.Q. points in one year is not uncommon. Let me point out here that I.Q. does *not* measure the innate capacity of a child to learn; it merely indicates the degree to which he is able to learn at that moment. After acquiring additional experience he may be able to learn much more at a more rapid rate.

A personal example serves to illustrate the point. In a school where I worked, certain I.Q. tests were administered to all transient children entering. After hearing a word and looking at a group of pictures, the child was expected to identify the object named. It became apparent after a short time that few deprived children could correctly identify the picture of a "counter." Why? Because there are few kitchen counters in the homes of economically deprived children. It was also obvious that few Negro children could identify "freckles" as called for on the test. These children were given lower I.Q. scores simply because they had not been exposed to the concepts being tested. In light of this information, can we say that low I.Q. scores indicate mental inferiority?

Can you imagine the bewilderment of an economically deprived child sitting in a first grade room where the teacher talks about the den—the lavatory—the dishwasher—the garbage disposal—the fireplace—the counter—the shower. These are words of the affluent. We often say that such a deprived child is stupid. Yet the experiences which a child has had prior to school entry can well determine his achievement rate regardless of his mental capacity.

How deprived is your child? Economically? Your answer—not at all. Experientially? Perhaps to a greater degree than you realize. If language is the key to mental development, then early and continuous language stimulation is important.

TALK TO YOUR CHILD

Words grow out of recognition of observable objects and actions. As children are taught to observe carefully, a greater foundation is laid for verbal expression. Growth in conversation and vocabulary stimulates further language ability and builds capacity for thinking.

A child who is seldom engaged in stimulating conversation is deprived. Too often parents are busy with their own world—attending meetings, parties, bridge clubs, working, relaxing, reading the newspaper—and the child is in the crib, bribed with a toy, sent outside, scolded for interrupting, or put in the care of a maid. These children are deprived. They need stimulating conversation. A parent who spends time with his child is saying to the child, "You are important." The parent who refuses to engage his child in meaningful dialogue says to the child that other things are more important than he. What does this behavior do to the child's self-perception? The child who feels good about himself, who readily and confidently enters into conversation, is more likely to achieve rapidly in school than the child who feels unimportant.

Talking with your child is important, but of equal importance is listening to him. When he talks, give him your full attention. This too helps him to know that he is important. Language takes two directions—receiving and transmitting. We receive when we listen and read. We transmit when we talk and write. A child needs to grasp this concept of language. Writing is talk put on paper. Let your child tell you a story; write it down in large letters, then read it back to him. This activity helps the child to understand the interrelatedness of talking and writing. Printed words are talk. As you read aloud to your child this fact may become obvious, but point it out anyway. Discuss the pictures. Pictures are important; they tell a story, and before learning to read words, children learn to read pictures.

DEVELOPING LISTENING SKILLS

In order to learn effectively a child must become a good listener, and the habit of listening can be taught him at an early age by parents who act consistently. The first step is to give simple directions to your child. Outline only one task to be accomplished at a time. As the child develops understanding, more than one task can be outlined consecutively, but clarity is important. Give directions, check to find out if directions are understood, then make sure that the directions are carried out. Say only what you mean. Never tell a child to perform a task unless you intend for it to be completed. There should be no exceptions. Clarity and consistency of directions help the child develop good listening habits, consistent behavior, and confidence in you and what you say. Words become more than sounds.

Many games can be devised to build good listening habits and to develop auditory discrimination. It is fun to describe to the child motions you want him to make and see if he can follow the directions: tell your child to take two steps forward—one step backward—touch his chin with one finger—close both eyes—place one foot behind the other—stand on one foot. Get two coins, two small wooden blocks, two glass marbles, and two spoons. With the child blindfolded tap like objects together and have him guess which objects made the sound.

You can design many games for developing auditory discrimination, but again I would point out that such games should fit naturally into the pattern of everyday living. They should not be designated as learning activities, separate from normal activities—learning is a natural part of life and should not be segregated. Children should be brought up to experience the joy of learning in everyday living.

To help your child develop intonation as well as listening skills, sing in different tones simple statements such as "Good morning," "How are you?" "I love you," and ask your child to repeat the statement in the same tone. After considerable practice even most monotones develop improved tonal discrimination.

Examples of games to develop listening skills could consume many pages, but half the fun of working (playing) with your child is in making up your own games. You can buy some excellent records for developing auditory discrimination, but remember, there is nothing more important than personal contact.

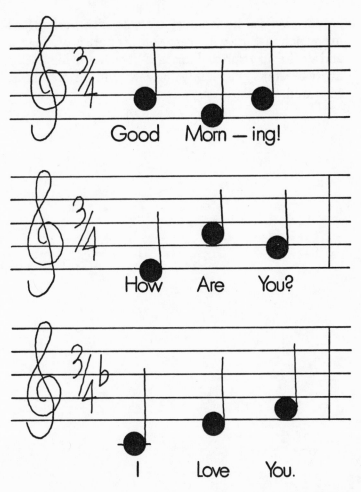

Good   Morn — ing!

How   Are   You?

I   Love   You.

To be an effective learner your child needs self-confidence. Self-confidence is not inherited; it is developed. The way in which you work with your child largely determines the degree of self-confidence he will maintain. You have heard many times the saying that success breeds success: you must arrange experiences for your child in a way that permits much more success than failure. In other words, don't make games so difficult or demanding that your child gets discouraged. As he goes from success to success with words and ideas, his capacity for further development is enhanced. Through proper exercise he will acquire extensive verbal facility, which in turn will create on his part a willingness and desire to express himself. When he achieves this expressiveness, his ability to learn will be greatly accelerated.

CHAPTER 5

Reading Readiness

Reading surely is one of the most important skills a child can acquire, yet an astonishing number of children fail to master this profoundly important art to the extent required for academic success and broad occupational choice. While it is possible to live without the capability of reading it is highly frustrating and exceedingly limiting in effect.

Schools in general have done a poor job of teaching children to read. Primarily, this failure can be attributed to neglect—colleges do not provide elementary teachers with the necessary skills for teaching reading adequately. Secondly, schools generally have not had the financial resources to obtain adequate materials; and thirdly, teachers generally lack the methods and managerial techniques to offer challenge and motivation to children with great variance in background (readiness skills) and ability.

Many educators will caution you against trying to

teach your child to read, but let me admonish you to not leave it all to the schools. I am not saying that you should teach your child to read before he enters the first grade, but you should make every reasonable effort to give him the prerequisite skills for reading and, when they are acquired, if he proceeds into the reading stage without urging, don't apologize. I would much rather have my child become bored because he already knew what was being taught than have him experience great frustration because he did not have the prerequisite skills for that which was being taught.

Several times I have witnessed preschool children saying to a teacher "Please teach me to read," or "I want to read"—and have seen the teacher refuse to provide instruction because she knew that no provision was made for readers at the beginning first-grade level. Refusing a child the opportunity to read when he is ready is just as bad as trying to force a child to read when he has insufficient background. No one has yet persuaded me to accept the argument that learning experiences for which children are ready should be withheld because they will be provided later. There are few times when it is detrimental for a child to know more than the majority of his classmates; children should be helped to acquire new skills and concepts at the moment they are ready and eager for them. Proponents of withholding learning experiences are in effect saying that all children are alike, that they learn all things at the same rate, and are all ready to learn the same things at the same time. I can't buy that philosophy. Children should be taught those things for which they have acquired the background.

READ TO YOUR CHILD

In reading, as in most other areas, the parent is the pace setter. If you yourself read a lot you are in effect saying to your child that reading is important and it is something you like to do. But how much more important reading becomes when you read to your child!

A child, even at age one, loves to have a parent read to him. Although he does not understand much that is being said, he loves the rhythm and modulation of the voice and he understands that reading is important. After all, Mommy or Daddy is doing this, and they are important people. At first the content is of little importance, but as the child begins to master a few words content becomes significant. Preschool storybooks are available in ever increasing numbers, but it is not necessary to have a new book each time you read to your child. Children love to hear familiar stories. How often have you had your child ask you to tell a familiar story again and again? Read stories to your child—not necessarily new stories—but read to him regularly. Many times reading itself is sufficient, but another important ingredient is discussion of the story—it is a grand opportunity to develop your child's comprehension and verbal facility.

Once your child exhibits interest in subjects where written material is available, don't limit your reading material to storybooks. My son, then three years old, had badly wanted to go with me on a trip to California, so when I returned I brought him a copy of a Disneyland booklet. He spent hours looking at the pictures, stopping only to say, "I want to go to Mickey Mouse." A few months later he saw a Disneyland special on TV and again he pored over the pictures in the well-worn booklet. When my youngest son was only in first grade and just beginning to read, he dearly loved a book about our nation's moon and space program which we purchased at a local service station. With each moon shot his interest was renewed, and on many occasions he asked me to read to him from the moon book. Reading is important, and you should express this fact to your child by reading to him regularly.

READINESS COMPONENTS

There are three basic ingredients in reading readiness. The first component, interest, was discussed above. The second is visual discrimination—the ability to differentiate between shapes, colors, sizes, etc. The third essential is auditory discrimination, the ability to distinguish between different sounds.

At first the only object most babies consistently recognize is their mother, and, although it is difficult to determine if recognition is initially gained through sight or sound, when recognition is gained, a milestone has been reached. Once your baby has accomplished this, he will achieve other discriminatory acts more rapidly, since, as you must have begun to guess, much learning is sequenced. By this I mean that most skills have prerequisites; that is, each skill learned is a foundation for a more advanced skill. The concept of prerequisites is what reading readiness is all about. No one can learn to read without having mastered certain lower-level skills, and to be sure that the child has these prerequisites you should personally see that he gets them.

Visual Discrimination

In helping your child to develop visual discrimination, familiar objects are most useful. Body parts are easily recognized—therefore, games can be played in which the child is asked to "show" his hand, eye, nose, or arm. As the child grows, matures, and acquires vocabulary, refinement in discrimination becomes possible and desirable. Now you may begin the use of smaller and less familiar objects. But never forget that the muscles of a preschool child's eye have not developed to the extent of permitting fine discrimination; therefore, objects which the child observes should be large enough to avoid eye strain. He will learn much faster if large objects are utilized.

There are certain concepts which your child should grasp as soon as he is capable, and whether or not he does will largely depend upon you. "Like" and "different" are important concepts. If you point out how things are alike in appearance and how they are different your child will soon understand what you are talking about. But don't expect him to see minute differences at first. After much experience with the terms "like" and "different" he will begin to apply them to how things are "alike" and "different" in the behavioral sense as well as the physical.

Here are some other important concepts that relate to size and position with which your child should become familiar: big—little, tall—short, large—larger—largest, small—smaller—smallest, fat—thin, long—short, up—down, over—under, in—out, beside—below—behind and next to. These descriptive words assist the child in following directions, which are important for reading readiness and for reading activities.

DEVELOPMENTAL GAMES

An excellent method of helping to develop your child's visual discrimination is through development tasks or games designed to teach particular skills and afford practice in their refinement. These games can be designed as single-concept activities or easily arranged in such a way that they become sequenced tasks with two or more learning levels included in each game, which will give the child an opportunity to proceed to the next level of learning once he has mastered the lower-level concept.

The developmental games found in this chapter are intended to stimulate your thinking and motivate you to design many and varied games yourself. Developmental games such as the following can be made from ordinary cardboard boxes; however, heavy poster board is neater and a little easier to use. Cut the cardboard into sizes that will just fit in large manila envelopes. Smaller pieces of cardboard can be placed in a regular 4¼-by-9½-inch envelope and the small envelope may be glued to the larger one for easy access and storage. On the big cardboard draw or paste a car, a dress, a rabbit, and a chair. On the small pieces of cardboard paste identical

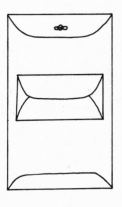

objects. The child simply matches like objects. When he can match identical objects with ease, he could proceed to matching different makes, models, or styles from the ones on the large card. Tasks can be made progressively more difficult. For example, the small matching cards may eventually show a bicycle (road transportation), trousers (clothing), a cow (animal), and a sofa (a seat). An even more advanced concept might include the matching of metal, wood, cloth, and fur to items on the large card of like composition. Although the last items do not altogether develop visual discrimination, you can include them to show how the concept of "like" and "different" can be developed and refined.

Basic Level

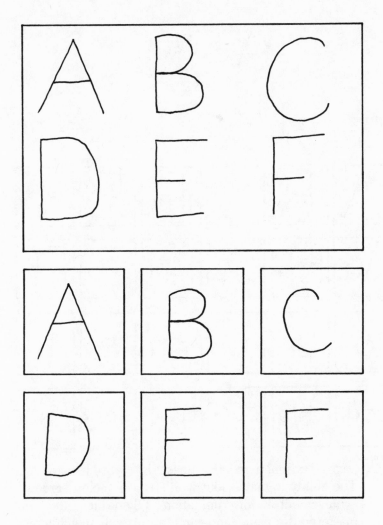

Another example of a single-concept developmental game involving visual discrimination is simply matching letters.

To make the above game into a sequence of games as shown on page 36, one can make additional small cards with lower- and upper-case letters, to be matched with the capitals on the large card. A higher level would include just lower-case letters, then finally words which begin with each letter found on the large card.

You can design developmental word games to teach your child further discrimination. In the example on

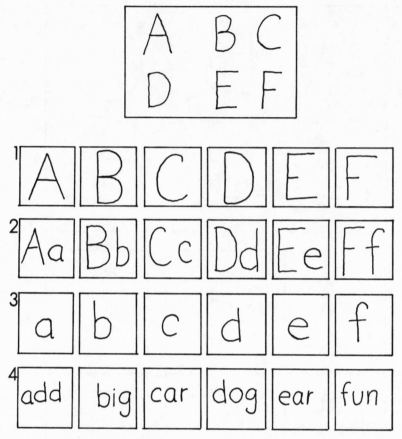

page 37, visual perception phases into word recognition. The ability to match like words is a notable degree of achievement in discrimination. When the child has mastered this game, and can also correctly match a picture to the corresponding printed symbol, he has demonstrated that he recognizes the word.

In making developmental games be sure to begin with easy, familiar objects. As your child makes correct responses don't dryly and unemotionally say, "That's right." Instead, show joyous and unrestrained approval. Make a big fuss over each success. Children need approval—they need to know that their actions please you. The exhibition of pleasure and excitement spurs a child to greater and more rapid achievements. Learning is exciting. You set the pattern for your child—be sure it is the right one.

Boy   Foot

Dog   Hand

Boy

Foot

Dog

Hand

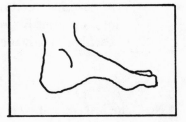

Word cards in large letters placed strategically can help your child toward word recognition. Small magnets glued to the back of word cards can easily be attached to the refrigerator door so that each time your child approaches the refrigerator words challenge him.

Attaching name cards to objects in the child's room is effective in word recognition and word meaning. For example, the word "bed" attached to the bed or a lamp labeled "lamp" can encourage word recognition. But let me warn you that plastering the house with words can be as bad as presenting no words at all. If the challenge is so great that mastery appears impossible, then your child will make little effort to rise to the challenge.

"But," you may say, "I believe in the phonetic approach to reading." So do I. But the time for concentrating on phonics can be delayed. Many children can best learn to read initially through the sight approach. Later, word attack skills can be strengthened through concentrating on sounds. But to concentrate on sounds at the very beginning frustrates many children and greatly retards their progress. A skilled and perceptive person can many times determine the right time for introducing sounds into the reading activities of a child, but you are not a reading teacher—you are helping your child to acquire readiness skills. One of these skills is visual discrimination: learning to recognize a few words is part of reading readiness. Few parents should venture into an intensive reading program which includes the teaching of advanced phonetic skills.

No "ONE" APPROACH TO READING

All children do not learn alike. Learning to read basically consists of breaking a code. Many children accomplish this step to reading through learning the sound of letters and letter blends, and most schools in the past have used the phonetic approach, utilizing a series of basal reading texts. This approach has been quite effective with the majority of children, but there is equal evidence that it is ineffective with many other children. Simply note the number of poor readers and nonreaders in almost any classroom in America. Year after year a child fails to find the key to reading success and year after year he is subjected to the same phonetic approach. When will people learn to accept what everyone knows—that individuals are different and must be taught differently? There *are* other effective approaches to reading.

Dr. Walter Barbe, a reading specialist of national prominence, was once driving his niece, who was in the second grade, home from school. He became aware that she was repeating what sounded like "so, no, lo, go, mo, ho" and "see, me, he, be, le, ge," and he asked her, "What are you doing?" With hardly a pause in her routine, the niece replied, "I'm sounding." A few moments later Dr. Barbe asked, "Are you practicing reading?" to which she curtly replied, "I said I am sounding." "Does sounding help you to read better?" he asked. "When I read, I read, and when I sound, I sound," came the persnickety answer. Sometimes a child sees the relationship between sounds and reading, and sometimes he doesn't. To provide no alternative ways of learning to read is indefensible and inexcusable.

LEARNING STYLES

Some children learn best through visual means, some through auditory, and still others through the kinesthetic sense—by touching. Perhaps you know the note-taker who remembers very little that he hears or reads but seldom forgets anything he has written down—this person is probably a kinesthetic learner. Several authorities agree that about twenty children in each one hundred fall into this category, yet almost no provision is made for kinesthetic learners. The wise parent and teacher takes this variance into consideration when preparing developmental games. If you don't know your child's learning style, why take a chance? Why not provide experiences appropriate to children with any learning style?

In preparing developmental games, especially those illustrated earlier which consisted of letters and letter combinations, use glue with sand, yarn, felt, or pipe clearners. Instead of merely writing the letters with a felt-tip pen, shape them by gluing a piece of yarn or pipe cleaner on cardboard. The child can now feel the letters in addition to seeing them. Felt letters can be purchased or cut out and glued to a piece of cardboard or placed on a flannel board.

An excellent kinesthetic game may be made by writing or drawing figures on cardboard with a tube of glue. If you wish to make the impression more pronounced, sprinkle the cardboard with sand before the glue dries. A sandpaper effect is achieved which accentuates the kinesthetic quality of the game.

We don't usually stop to consider the contribution of the different senses to the reading process. We forget that one child may make much greater use of a given sense than another child. When one sense is underdeveloped a child often compensates by developing another sense to an unusual degree, as is vividly illustrated by the deaf child who said to her mother as they went to bed, "Don't turn off the light because I can't hear what you say." Likewise the child who depends on touch to a large extent is greatly handicapped in learning to read through the usual visual approach. Don't ignore the possibility that your child may learn best through one of the other senses.

AUDITORY DISCRIMINATION

Hearing a sound and being able to associate that sound with a letter or combination of letters is crucial to reading success. The sounding of words, as described in Walter Barbe's story about his niece, is a good approach to helping your child. Give examples of rhyming words and ask him to say as many rhyming words as he can. Select simple words which will be easy for him. It really doesn't matter if many of the words are nonsense words because the same objective can be accomplished. Don't persist in this activity (or any other activity) until the child tires. Overexercise can destroy an appetite for the game. It is much better to leave the child still wanting to play more.

As the child masters rhyming words, he will develop the background to determine words which begin alike. You can say a word, then ask your child to say as many words as he can which begin like the word you named. Naming words which begin alike is a rather high-level skill and therefore difficult for most children until they have mastered many of the skills taught by the developmental games described earlier in this chapter.

Finding pictures of objects which begin with the same letter, or pointing out such objects, is an even higher-level skill than naming words which begin alike. This activity is appropriate only for a limited number of children prior to the time they enter school, but if your child obviously has the prerequisite skills for it, then it perhaps should be included in his repertoire of games.

There are lots of games for developing this skill. As an example, you might make an 8-by-11-inch card with four different letters, as illustrated on page 42. Cut small cards (4-by-4) and paste or draw on these cards pictures of several objects which begin with the letters found on the larger card. Have the child match the picture to the appropriate letter on the big card.

The child who is learning to read needs a wealth of experiences, both to increase his speaking vocabulary and to give him an extensive background for understanding and enjoying what he reads.

Experiences do not necessarily have to be first hand. Television is an excellent medium for them. It should not be used exclusively as a teaching tool, but it can make a significant contribution. While it is impossible for most preschool-age children to visit such places as Africa, Canada, Alaska, or the Florida Everglades, televison frequently can take them there. Television is a great "equalizer" in that all children, regardless of economic status or social position, can encounter similar experiences through the television medium.

Children rarely have the opportunity to observe numerous animals in their natural habitat, but television can make this experience possible, and will furnish

A B
C D

apple
ant
acorn

boy
boat
ball

cat
car
cup

dog
doll
dress

narration that makes the observations meaningful. Scientific feats, such as moon landings and exploration; holiday celebrations; political activities which will be recorded in history—all these are rich, vicarious experiences with which television provides a youngster.

The children's educational television programs that have emerged in recent years are proving to be of great value in teaching children certain reading and numerical skills. A three-year-old friend of mine, who is a regular viewer of one such program, has learned to recognize numerous words and should be able to read quite well prior to entering school. In addition to the purely educational programs, there are programs which are primarily entertaining in nature, yet include educational activities. Even some of the Saturday-morning cartoons have added brief spots designed to teach designated reading or reading-prerequisite skills.

A few mature preschoolers enjoy informative adult programs. Recently, I was on a television talk show called "Coffee with Judy," discussing activities for preschool-age children. When the program ended, one of the participants told me that her five-year-old daughter insisted on watching "Coffee with Judy" daily instead of watching a television nursery-school program on a competing channel.

Your child is a unique individual and should be treated as one when you direct his television experiences. As the person most responsible for directing his activities you often should watch programs with him so that you can talk with him about it afterwards, and design follow-up activities for him to do. It is great to have an enjoyable experience, but how much better it is if it can be shared with someone!

Television has much to offer children provided parents are selective in its use, but it was never intended to be a baby sitter, and if you allow it to be one, you are misusing both it and your child.

Talking with your child, reading stories, telling stories, making up stories together, taking walks, and visiting interesting places, both in person and through viewing television, are all equally as important as making developmental games available to the child. In all the activities described some children will progress more rapidly than others. The chances are great that your child will move rapidly from simple activities to those increasingly difficult. However, I must caution you to avoid forcing your child into activities for which he is unprepared. Above all, make the activities exciting and enjoyable for both you and your child.

CHAPTER 6

Number Concepts

Math begins with objects, not numerals. Numerals are needed for accelerating work with number concepts and for transmitting mathematical ideas, but numerals are abstractions and therefore difficult to grasp. Even when equipped with knowledge of this fact, most teachers and parents have an almost uncontrollable urge to start children working with pencil and paper, making ones, twos, threes, and fours and adding them together. Thus mathematics becomes an abstract subject.

For a child to acquire adequate mathematics skills it is imperative that his number concepts be well grounded in concrete representations. Most math concepts, when thoroughly understood, can be illustrated through the use of concrete objects. If you plan to help your child develop the prerequisite skills for success in first-grade mathematics, let me encourage you to use manipulative objects extensively. The kinds of objects you use are unimportant. Bottle caps, pebbles, popsicle sticks, buttons, or other objects will do if they are small enough to manipulate easily and the child is mature enough to handle them safely. The point is that concrete objects for counting, for making groups, and for regrouping are important. After the child understands the addition concept through using objects, he then has one of the prerequisites for adding with numerals. Many children can add and subtract on paper, yet have little understanding of what they are really doing. These children often go all the way through school memorizing number facts and rules; but when faced with a simple, everyday problem they become completely confused because they don't understand what is involved in finding the solution.

SEEING THE SOLUTION

In order to solve math problems effectively, a person must be able to visualize the problem and the process involved in its solution. As a child struggles with a math problem his entire countenance changes as the solution becomes clear. If you are looking into the eyes of a youngster, you can readily perceive when he "sees" the solution. This ability to "see" is accomplished through the use of manipulative devices, so that the child can clearly visualize the mathematical concepts involved. As a child adds two additional objects to a group which already contains four like objects, he can literally see that two added to four makes six. This process of using objects is much more meaningful than memorizing that the numeral two when added to the numeral four represents six. Certainly the latter must be learned, but only after the additive concept involved in putting objects together is thoroughly understood and can be visualized easily.

Words and numerals are merely symbols. For example, the word "four" is of little value without the four-ness concept. To teach the concept of four, four objects are needed. Four small pebbles, four sticks, four ABC blocks, or even four people will suffice. The important thing is that there are four tangible objects—objects which can be seen and touched. A child needs many experiences with four prior to the time he starts writing the numeral. Through the moving of objects he can be shown that one and three are four; that two and two are four; that three and one are four; and that one, and one, and one, and one are four. This awareness can be accomplished without the use of a written numeral. Later the child can be introduced to the symbol which represents four. On the other hand, learning to count by rote is acceptable at any stage of number development provided it is followed by concrete experiences to develop understanding.

SETTING THE STAGE

When a baby begins to talk, the stage is set for number concept development. Concepts such as big, little, large, larger, largest, small, smaller, smallest, over, under, behind, below, top, bottom, beside, beneath, up, down, longer, shorter, same, and different are important for understanding and working with numbers. Conversing with your child can help him develop this vocabulary as experiences are planned and leisurely introduced. Simple objects, like the pebbles, sticks, or blocks mentioned earlier, can be compared and placed in different positions to illustrate the above concepts.

Many developmental games cannot be readily classified by subject area. This is as it should be—adults seldom utilize learning from one subject area exclusively. Furthermore, precision in defining the area of development is not imperative so long as positive development is taking place. For example, many readiness experiences for mathematics are closely related to readiness for reading. The developmental game which follows—matching of shapes—develops visual perception, and visual perception is vital to reading readiness as well as math readiness. This game is played by matching the shape cutouts to the shapes on the card.

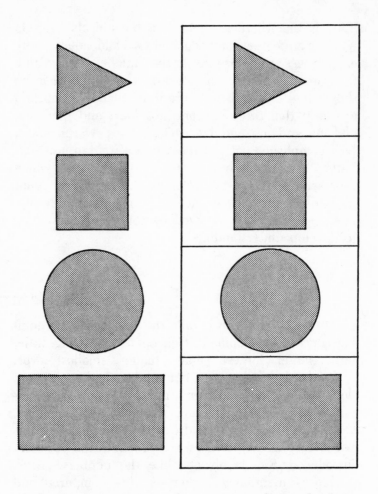

Visual perception is also very much involved in matching numeral cutouts with numeral outlines.

CIGAR-BOX FLANNEL BOARD

An excellent resource for teaching math concepts is a cigar box and an assortment of felt shapes, figures, and numerals. Sheets of felt can be purchased at most school-supply stores and at many variety stores. The lid of a cigar box can be covered with flannel to make a small flannel board. The assorted felt items can be stored in the box and taken out, as needed, to illustrate number concepts. Felt will adhere to flannel, making it easy to maintain the positions of figures. Shapes such as squares, circles, triangles, rectangles, and trapezoids can be cut from sheets of felt and placed in the cigar box. Plus, minus, and equal signs should also be included. Certainly all single-digit numerals including the zero are a must.

There are many ways of using this math kit. You can select a shape or a numeral and ask your child to display the same shape or numeral on the small flannel board. Or you may, depending upon the achievement level of your child, merely say, "Show me a square." As the child acquires additional concepts, you may ask for a certain number of different shapes along with their names. You may place a numeral on the board and ask your child to show that number of objects. You may reverse this process by placing a given number of objects on the board and asking your child to respond by selecting the numeral which represents the number of objects.

For children who have acquired the prerequisite skills, math problems can be worked or illustrated on the flannel board. Easy problems such as $\bullet \bullet + \bullet \bullet = \underline{\quad}$ or $2 + 2 = \underline{\quad}$ can be used. The solutions may be illustrated by placing two squares and two more squares

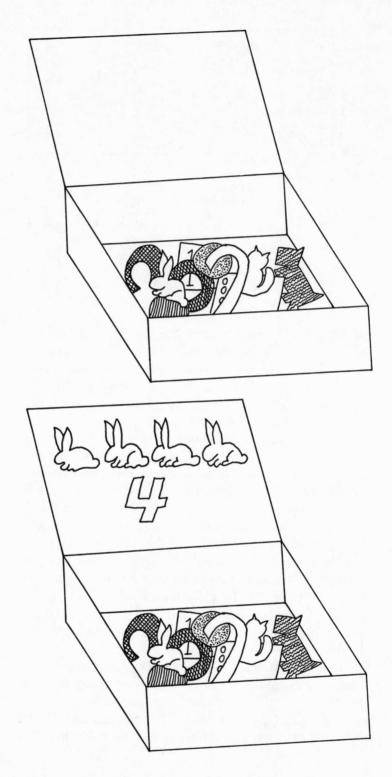

on the board, then combining the squares and counting them. These are only a few of an unlimited number of uses for the cigar math-resource box. You will think of many more uses immediately.

A deck of cards is one of the most useful tools for teaching mathematics on levels from preschool readiness to statistical probability. Children can learn to match colors, shapes, and numerals. Any combination of the above, such as black fours, can be used as criteria for matching. Cards can be used to teach numeral recognition, counting, addition and subtraction. With a little ingenuity numerous card games can be devised which will make the learning of math concepts fun.

NUMBER GAMES

Developmental games for math readiness may be designed as single-concept games such as the first two

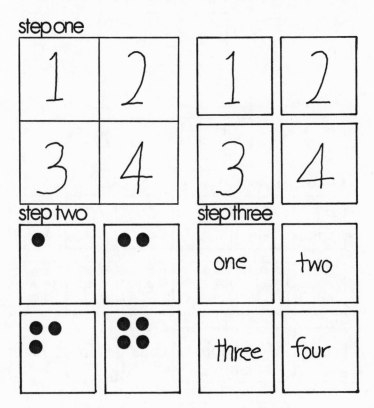

math illustrations, or they may be designed as multiple-concept games with the lower-level games providing the prerequisite skills for succeeding levels.

With a felt-tip pen or magic marker, divide a piece of poster board or cardboard, approximately 8½ by 11 inches, into four equal rectangles. Write the numerals 1, 2, 3, and 4 in sequence from left to right. Prepare smaller cards with identical numerals for matching to the numerals on the large card. The child simply matches numeral to numeral at this level.

A higher-level concept can be taught by using small cards with dots of appropriate number for matching with the numerals on the large card. Finally, the words one, two, three, and four can be written on small cards for matching with the numerals. The latter level is quite advanced for many preschool children, for it

4	3	5
1	6	2
2	1	3
4	6	5

Make two of each:

1	2	3	4	5	6

•	• •	• • •	• • • •	• • • • •	• • • • • •

one	two	three	four	five	six

involves word recognition as well as number recognition; so adjust your expectations according to the skills your child has previously acquired. If, however, any level of this game seems too easy for him, it can be made more difficult by adding more numerals and by breaking the sequence. Additional small cards bearing numerals, dots, and words can be made for matching.

Take care that the dots are placed on the cards as illustrated. This arrangement makes it easy to teach the concept of odd and even—if there is a leg, the number is odd; if there is no leg, the number is even.

THE KINESTHETIC LEARNER

Consideration of the different learning styles of children is as important in math as in reading, and appropriate materials are much more readily available. Manipulative objects and flannel board cutouts are excellent for the kinesthetic learner as well as for children with other learning styles. To make developmental games more appropriate for the kinesthetic learner, numerals, dots, and words can be made with Elmer's Glue or a similar brand of glue. Sand or small decorator gravel may be sprinkled on the wet glue, or the glue may be permitted to dry without adding the sandpaper effect. The degree of your child's sensitivity to touch will dictate the effect needed.

Raised numerals are excellent for use with children who have certain learning disabilities. Your child may learn best through touch; so why take a chance? Use some kinesthetic materials intermittently.

To make sandpaper numerals you will need ten six-by-six-inch cards and several pieces of sandpaper (or Elmer's Glue and sand). Using numeral patterns, make one of each single-digit numeral by tracing on the sandpaper and cutting out with scissors. Glue one sandpaper numeral to each card. Collect a box of bottle caps or buttons.

Illustrate to your child the use of the tips of the first

two fingers for "writing" the numerals. Begin with "0" and trace it with the two finger tips. Explain that the "0" means "not any."

Now, place the "1" card next to the "0" card. Say "one" as you do this. Help your child trace it with his finger tips and say, "One"; then place a bottle cap or a button at the bottom of the card to show that the numeral "one" means "one object." As your child masters the preceding numerals, continue with the other numerals, tracing with finger tips and placing objects. A variation would be to turn the cards over, then let your child draw one numeral at a time and ask him to place the appropriate number of objects below the numeral. But don't overdo it. Never let the child become weary before stopping. Leave him with an appetite for more.

Some parents, made insecure by the introduction of modern math in elementary schools, tend to shy away from teaching number concepts to their children for fear of teaching them wrongly. But the primary aim of modern math is to teach children to understand our number system, so, in helping your child and in encouraging him to develop number skills, don't worry about conflict with modern math. If you use concrete objects which your child can manipulate in his games, and if you stress understanding rather than rote memorization, both of you will profit enormously.

Numbers are fascinating. As Jerome Bruner says, "Any subject can be taught effectively in some intellectually honest form to any child at any stage of development." Number concepts can be taught to the very young, yet they can challenge the genius of well-schooled adults. Numbers range from the fractional part to the infinite. Numerals can be placed side by side in any sequence in a never ending progression yet continue to have meaning to the mind capable of comprehending at that level. Alluding to the infinity of numbers, someone once said, "I want you as a friend—not like the alphabet, but like numbers which never end."

CHAPTER 7

Classifying

Classification is a basic skill which aids in problem solving and independent thinking. Organization in our lives is made possible by our ability to classify. Your house could serve well as the laboratory for a study in classification. For example, pots and pans have a proper place in the kitchen. The utensils are grouped together, yet separated into certain categories. Your clothing has been organized into categories in drawers and closets. The basis for such classification is the ability to see the way objects, ideas, or entities relate—how they are alike or how they are different.

In the chapter "Begin at the Beginning," a child's growing awareness of the world was discussed. His senses experienced and his mind stored away many bits of information. He is now ready to use this information. If you have implemented the ideas for developmental games in the preceding chapters on numbers and reading readiness, you have already begun play involving classification.

COLOR-SHAPE-SIZE GAME

When you cut out colored shapes and let your child sort them, he was classifying. If you made these shapes referred to on page 48 all one color, a match could be made by shape—triangle to triangle, square to square, circle to circle, and rectangle to rectangle. If you will expand this game now, you can follow the multilevel developmental game idea, proceeding on to a more difficult level. Make two more sets of the same shapes, each set a different color. Give them to your child and ask him to sort them into the groups that go together. If he uses the shape classification, putting all like shapes together, ask him if there is any other way that he can group them. You might even have to say, "Could you look at the color instead of the shape?" The third level would be to cut another set of the same shapes, one in each of the three colors, but making this set either larger or smaller than the original set. Now the game would be to see how many different ways you could put these into groups. When a grouping has been made at each level, you will want to ask the question, "How are these alike now? How are they different?" For instance, all of the blues are alike, but they are different shapes. At the third level you may need to ask the question, "Could you put all the large shapes together, and the small ones?" "How is each pile different from the other now?" There are many other ways to apply this idea, too.

BUTTON GAMES

You can also play a categorization game using the button collection mentioned in the preceding chapter. If you store your buttons in a tin with fitted top, let your child cover it with contact paper and glue one or two bright buttons on the top. If you use a cardboard box, ask your child to decorate it with tempera paint or original pictures cut out and glued on the top and sides. Then getting out the buttons will be more like play. A playing board or box could be quite useful. With cardboard sections, make compartments in a cigar box to facilitate the sorting process. To make compartments, cut cardboard—one strip the length of the box (dimension a) and two the width of the box (dimension b), making the strips not quite as wide as the box is high (dimension c). Mark the long strip into three equal sections and cut the marks to within one inch of the top of the strip. Mark the two short strips in the middle and cut within one inch of the bottom of the strips. Set the short strips down on the long strips interlocking at the slits and place in the box. A muffin tin, an egg carton or an ice tray (plastic ones would be especially good) could fill the same purpose as the cigar box.

In categorizing buttons, employ the same techniques you used in playing the game of color-shapes. As your child divides the buttons into different groups, ask him how they are alike and how they are different. Ask leading questions to suggest other possibilities. Notice if he applied the principles of the color-shape game to the button game. This transfer of learning is tremendously important. Did he use all the categories for sorting that were employed before? Color, size, shape? How many other possibilities does he think of? How many can you think of and suggest? Some possibilities to start with are composition (wood, cloth, plastic), tactile sense (smooth, rough), by holes (some buttons have four holes, some have two holes, some one hole, some with a metal ring on the bottom and no hole), by suitability—which is of course subjective—(for girls, for boys, for ladies or men, for dressy clothes, for play clothes), or by use (some for games, for markers). Buttons lend themselves beautifully to this activity, but there are many other appropriate objects. You can use everyday objects in your house; in fact, you should do that to encourage the transfer of learning to take place in the world of experience.

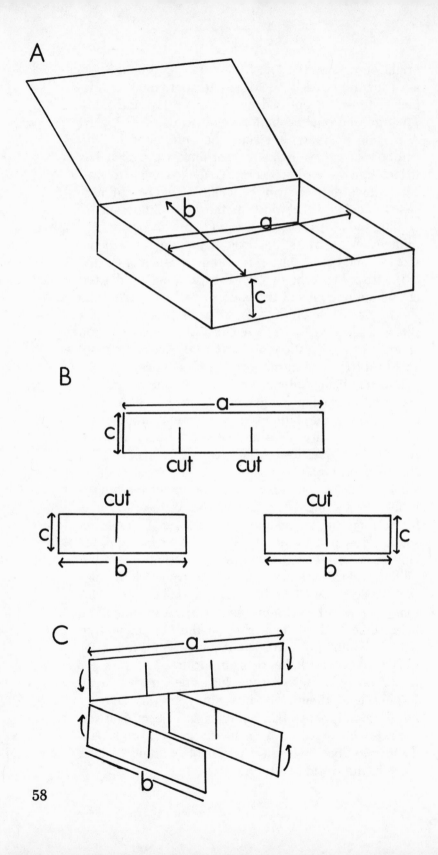

A

B

C

58

A teacher whom I observed was once working with a group of four-year-olds, and asked six of the children to sit in a tight circle with their feet in the middle. Then she asked them to look at their shoes and see how many ways they could say their shoes were alike, and after they exhausted those possibilities. she asked them how many ways they could say their shoes were different.

Your house and your yard hold infinite classification possibilities, and exploring them will contribute to your purpose and to the spirit of fun. The buttons were a categorization activity using like objects and pointing out as many ways as possible to group them within this one category— buttons. When your child has mastered this skill, you will want to move on to a different type of grouping, involving more than one object—such as items in a department store. Keep in mind the basic goal—planning activities or creating opportunities for your child to "see" objects, and later abstractions, and to determine how they can and do go together to suit the purpose of the moment or to solve problems. Do these things "go together" in the way that I need them to?

STORE GAME

Making a store game is a very good next choice. Using a large sheet of paper, ask your child to imagine a big, tall store with an elevator that is about to make a stop on each floor. Now get him to tell you what kind of items are on each floor. Children who have been shopping often will probably do this easily, but if your child has had limited experience you will need to be prepared to ask those leading questions again. His responses will be your categories.

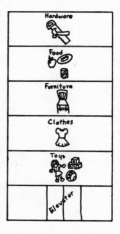

Line off the floors on the paper and label them as in the illustration at right. Now find a stack of old magazines, and together cut out pictures of items in the groups he named. To make the game durable, paste each picture you cut out on a piece of cardboard—optimum size about 2½ by 4 inches. (When your child cuts these out he will be giving exercise to small muscles, and the size of the card will be large enough for him to see but not too large for small hands.) First play a simple grouping game—mix up the cards, then lay them on the correct floor. Later you could introduce a beanbag throw—playing a card appropriate to the floor on which the bag lands. You can divide the cards and take turns playing, reserving half the cards for a draw pile. If you can't play you must draw a card. The first one to play all his cards wins.

If this game is fun for your child, you can continue to exercise the multiple-level idea by dividing each floor into subgroups: toys (vehicle toys, wind-up toys, dolls), clothes (boys, girls, men, women), furniture (lamps, tables, chairs, or by rooms). In using this game with mothers of preschool children, I have found it to be very popular. One mother came back after several days for a new "store." Her children had worn out the original store after three days of play. We stapled the new one inside a plastic dry-cleaning bag to protect it.

TYPES OF CATEGORIZATION

The button game involved one kind of object sorted by various attributes. The store game uses many different objects but puts them into a few predetermined categories (the floors). In this respect the button game called for more original thinking than the store game, in much the same way as a discussion test calls for more information than a true-false test which requires only that you sort out into already determined groups of true or false. However, the store game requires the ability to generalize in broad categories. The first floor was for toys, and the child must have the understanding that a teddy bear, a wagon, a rubber car, and a ball are all different, in that they are made of different materials and are of entirely different sizes, but that they are also alike, in that they are all toys or are things with which to play.

As your child begins to venture into the realm of abstract thinking, it would be a good idea to give him some practice in conceptualization. A *Go-Together Book* does the job well. Using blank paper, make a booklet by stapling the left side together or by using paper brads or safety pins. Cut from a magazine pictures which your child will recognize and which can be easily categorized. Select only one picture in each category. For instance, you might choose one picture of food, one of clothing, one of a toy, and one of transportation items. Glue or paste one picture on the top of each blank page. Give the book to your child with an old magazine and suitable scissors. Ask him to finish the book by cutting out other pictures that go with the picture that you have already pasted on the page. You might increase his interest by doing only one page a day. When he finishes a page, ask him to tell you how the pictures go together. If he has a reason, he is right. Perhaps you pasted a blue dress on one page thinking other items of clothing could be added to it. Your child might do just that—using items of clothing for any family member, only ladies' clothing, perhaps only other dresses. But suppose he used not clothing, but other blue things? If he says that he added other items because they too were blue, then they do go together in that respect. If you used a table to suggest the furniture category, what other possibilities might your child come up with? Perhaps he will look at that page, see four legs on the table, and cut out pictures of things with four legs. Great! Maybe he will add pictures of other things made of wood, furniture or otherwise. Great again! You are accomplishing your purpose so long as your child is able to give you a reason why the pictures "go together."

TRANSFER OF LEARNING

These games may bring your child to the realization that any given item can belong to many groups. Encourage this awareness. The application of classifying is that of providing organization to everyday living, a skill we use almost constantly. Ideas and concepts can also be classified. Good and bad can become categories, as can long and short. Both are relative. However, beyond this ability to classify things (seeing a relationship and putting things together on that basis) lies the skill of seeing new relationships in the realm of objects and ideas. The application of understanding to such a new situation is what we call transfer of learning, and this kind of problem solving is a major goal of education. In a problem solving situation, we bring some understanding or learning to bear upon a new situation in a way that eliminates the problem.

Through classifying comes the ability to recognize new possibilities and new relationships. There is a truly creative element in the skill of classifying.

CHAPTER 8

Creativity

Creativity is the word our parents used to describe what we now facetiously call doing our own thing— exercising our own special combination of skills, innate abilities, educated tastes, and imagination. As you consider, plan and implement activities to help your children, creativity is an area that deserves your full consideration.

The children of the sixties and seventies have made a real contribution by their emphasis on their "own thing." It has helped to broaden my understanding of what creativity actually is or could be, and perhaps it has done the same for you. When creativity is mentioned, do you immediately think of ability in the area of the fine arts? Generally we have allowed painters, dancers, writers, and poets a monopoly in our thinking about the area of creativity for quite long enough. Not that they did anything to limit us; we limited ourselves in this respect. Maybe when Sputnik first appeared, and science became exciting, thinking and acting creatively were projected into other areas. Painting, dancing, and writing are very creative skills, absolutely so; but any interest can be creative. Whether or not it becomes so is largely a matter of training and attitude.

When you cook, do you use the same few recipes and menus day after day, or do you try new ones and invent one occasionally? Do you always buy "outfits" for yourself and your child, or can you mix and match? Perhaps you cook what your family likes rather than taking a chance on something new, or buy outfits only because it is easier or faster or more economical. Fine. But somewhere along the line, in some area, you exercise more individuality, don't you? You inject *you* into your activity. Maybe if you considered it more carefully, you could do so to a greater extent or in more areas. This is where to begin in helping your child develop creativity—by your example. When creativity is mentioned, do you think of some special activity requiring unusual efforts or talent? To set a creative example you just have to be you, to know who "you" are, and you have to be busily engaged in being that person. If individuality is "the unique sum of the characteristics or qualities that set one person apart from others," then creativity is what happens, what results from the operation of that unique sum of characteristics. Creativity is that particular set of abilities, thoughts, and ideas in motion.

It may be necessary to convince some people that creativity is important. Modern education, and even this book, has placed emphasis on helping children to learn more rapidly and more fully. It has been established to our satisfaction that rapid acquisition of knowledge is a desirable thing, but only if we sufficiently acknowledge and include the area of creativity. Nobody wants to raise a robot—not even a very smart, efficient robot. The most notable criticism of some very efficient educational approaches is that they accelerate the accumulation of facts, leaving the child and his purposes behind.

To prevent even a minor version of the mistake of resorting to rote learning, you perhaps have already begun to set the example for creative behavior by making and using the games in the preceding chapters. Making games from materials you have handy is setting a creative example in a very uncomplicated way. Doing things with simplicity is a plus factor. It is the uncomplicated, daily example that makes sufficient impact to become incorporated into your child's thinking and behavior. This is why it is so important to start with you and your thinking.

Are you willing, able, and secure enough to be you? I am not trying to suggest a disregard for the opinions of others, but merely to ask whether you respect yourself as much as you respect what others think of you and your ideas. Are you willing, able, and secure enough to let your child be himself? I believe that lack of security is the most formidable opponent of creativity in children. Children are often so busy doing and being what we want them to be, that they don't have the time or the nerve to be themselves.

Creativity is first an attitude—a positive concept. We have to dare to expose our ideas, our dreams and the products of our imagination. Overcontrol and overdirection of children is the enemy of creativity. Some children literally want Mommy or Daddy to tell them what to think and what to want—there is little chance for creativity to develop there.

Utilize every opportunity to let your young child exercise independence. Naturally you will use your good judgment. I'm not an advocate of overpermissiveness by any means, but when a child can choose his own clothes, let him! It doesn't have to be the very combination you would have chosen every time, does it? Apply this attitude to as many daily activities as possible. Often sheer habit prompts us to do things for our children long after they are able to assume the responsibility for that action or decision themselves. The opportunity for independence leads to early development of confidence; when readiness, ability, and opportunity match, the confident child is willing to be creative. He is the one who will dare to paint the picture and voice the idea.

SEE YOUR CHILD

Having considered the atmosphere in which creativity develops best, how can you expedite or nourish the process? First of all, look at your child and really see him: every person, young and old, has some special areas in which he has flair or inborn natural feelings. Your child's special areas will not necessarily be ones in which your talents or even your interests lie, so be prepared to appreciate skills you did not achieve or even understand. Watching your child, considering him, and observing his areas of special abilities is fascinating —don't miss this joy. Anything that cultivates an increased respect for your child, as this kind of observation should, is valuable. He has some special talent or facility that neither parent may recognize yet, but do be on the lookout for it and give it a climate to thrive in.

WRITING AND ACTING

You can encourage the emergence of special skills with all kinds of activities and games. Try making an *All about Me* book, which can be very stimulating and satisfying. With several blank pages of inexpensive paper, ask your child to cut pictures from magazines, draw pictures, and dictate stories that are all about himself—what he likes to do, eat, play, wear, what he looks like, and where he lives. Helping him make such a book does several things beside stimulate language. It gives him a chance to stop and think about things. It tells him that you are interested in knowing these things too, all of which contributes to the development of his positive self-image.

For older preschool children a good game for devel-

oping self-image and confidence is "Let's Be on TV."
You will need a large cardboard box, turned on its side
so that your child can get inside. Cut out a square in the
middle of the side opposite the entrance, leaving at
least a six-inch margin on three sides and a much larger
margin at the bottom. This opening will form the TV
screen. Now suggest that your child or he and his
friends do a show. If they watch television they will
probably be familiar with a particular show after which
they can pattern their activity. If the "program" is musical, encourage the use of musical instruments. How
many different ones can he make or simulate? Invite
other children to get into the act. Each child can have a
turn, and when they are not on stage can be the audi-
ence. If music is not their line—or if they tire of that
version of the game—suggest that they pair up and act
out stories—original ones preferably, but beginning
with an old favorite might get things off to a good start.
If the action gets lively, your TV screen will be too
small, so suggest a move to a larger area.

A "dress-up" box might enhance the spirit of play.
Put old or torn dresses, trousers, jackets, shoes, purses,
hats, and jewelry in a handy box for such use. The children will probably enjoy performing in these outfits,
and if they forget the show and simply cavort or enjoy
role-playing in your clothes, they are imagining and
acting out what it would be like to be grown-up—to be
like you. This development of imagination is an aspect
of creativity.

If your child doesn't respond to the idea of performing on TV, or if he seems too self-conscious to enjoy it,
you might begin with puppets and work up to a live
performance.

THE PUPPET SHOW

Much has been written about the successful use of
puppets to encourage self-expression. They are fun,
too. You can make numerous kinds of puppets: sock
puppets, paper-bag puppets, popsicle-stick and finger-

face puppets. For our consideration all of them are good. The kind with which I have had the best luck is the sock puppet which slips on over the child's hand as illustrated: the tip of the sock-toe fits over the tip of the four

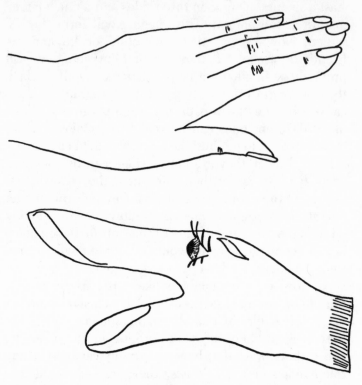

fingers of the child's hand; the heel fits over the tip of the thumb and the bottom of the foot stretches across the palm of the hand and tucks back in the fold made when the thumb and opposing fingertips touch. By moving his fingers and thumb the child makes the puppet "talk." Any face you wish to make is drawn, painted, or sewn on the portion of the sock that fits across the top side of the child's fingers and hand. The paper or plastic-bag puppet is one that your child can make himself. The face can be drawn on the bag with magic marker so that the mouth will be located in the fold of the bag to achieve a talking effect when your child slips his hand inside the bag. However, I have found this type pup-

pet to be a little more difficult for a child to manage.

As your child's small muscles develop and finer control is possible, you will find that drawing faces on ice-cream spoons, tongue depressors, or popsicle sticks is fun and makes a quick supply of puppets for an original puppet play. Don't let your child become bogged down in the mechanics of the activity. Any way he chooses to implement the puppet idea is fine—you are encouraging his creativity when you initiate dramatic play.

I have mentioned several games to encourage development of your child's imagination, and by now you may be saying, "My child's imagination is already over-developed!" In the normal developmental sequence, a child will become quite imaginative sometime between the ages of three and four years. He imagines that lions and tigers are under his bed and that a giant is lurking down the street. At this age fairy tales and fables give the child an outlet for his imaginative activity and a focus for his fears. The opportunity to exercise imagination is important to the development of a creative child. Don't accept his fanciful statements as intentions to express literal truths, and don't interpret this natural development as a sign that your child's imagination must be curbed. Use a little humor: "My, what a story! How exciting, tell me more!" If you pounce on his imaginative suggestions with severity he may learn something you didn't intend to teach: imagination is a no-no! You do want him to leave the lions and tigers behind eventually, but you also want to keep his imagination intact so that it may grow and develop further.

Creativity operates in the realm of the imagination. In fact, the two are so closely related that it is difficult to discuss them separately. Imagination is the dream, creativity the result, and the two are parted only with difficulty. At conception, creativity is imagination,

69

only later does it produce results. Scientists and inventors are as creative as composers and authors. They all put known quantities together in unique ways, whether it be scientific facts that lead to a new discovery or musical notes that make a new song.

To prepare our children to engage in creative activities, we must not limit them to the way things *are*. We need to encourage them to live in reality but also to exercise their imagination and envision things as they might be—to try things out and see what results. Children don't come to us as artists or inventors or even as creative people; they come with potential. They start in small ways, and with our help and encouragement they exercise their imagination. Large accomplishments begin small.

I see potential for budding creativity in unlikely places everywhere I look. Do you? Recently my daughter and her friend were swimming with inner tubes. They noticed that the tubes were of various sizes. As I watched, they stacked them three high, putting the largest on the bottom, smallest on top, and then mounted them to ride and play in the water. I had never seen inner tubes used in this way and neither had they, but it was fun! Earlier my son had watched several sailboats in the lake where he was swimming. They caught his eye and his fancy. He had at hand a small plastic play boat, barely large enough to hold him. Yet, after he found just the right two sticks, a torn sheet, and a ball of cord, he rigged up a sail and somehow managed to sail that contraption half the afternoon. Swimming with tubes and sailing plastic boats may be just "child's play," but imagination develops in such situations.

As you play with your child, let him know you enjoy his original efforts. When you encourage creative play, you are helping your child to put his imagination to work.

REMOVE LIMITATIONS

One subtle way parents may discourage creativity is by insisting that there is only one way to play a game

—or do anything for that matter. Does it have to be played just one way—"the way"—your way? There are some situations in which there is only one reasonable way to proceed, true enough. There are also many situations in which our way, "the way," the way that seems right and natural to us, is not the only, or even the most desirable, way. As often as possible let your child follow his inclinations. Make it a point to use play materials in different ways. The developmental games of other chapters have many possibilities. These activities encourage alternate suggestions from your child when he knows that variations are acceptable to you. Respond to his suggestions with enthusiasm and encourage more of the same.

Toys Are for Play

Your choice of toys and play materials for your child will be significant. Avoid or limit what I term the performing toys that leave nothing for the child and his imagination to do. Toys are to play with—not watch! If there were ever a contest for the perfect toy, I believe I would vote for blocks. Blocks provide hours of fun for children as well as opportunities for growth and practice in almost every area of child development: physical exercise, small motor control, eye-hand coordination, language, and number concepts, as well as imaginative play. In making your selection of toys, remember to consider their play value and the opportunity they might provide for exercising the imagination.

Let a good portion of the play material you provide be items which your child can use—the raw material with which to do other things. You will do well to consider the possibilities of articles in your house. Many children have a natural curiosity about how things work. They are the children who don't play with their toys; they take them apart instead. All children may do this to some extent, but some children have a much deeper or more intense curiosity along this line. If your child is

71

one of these, you know just what I mean! He observes closely everything of a mechanical nature with which he comes in contact. The nuts and bolts are always missing from his pegboard desk or workbench. Construction toys appeal to him. He would rather take the screws out of toys than to play with the toys in the way they were intended.

I have seen mothers and fathers fuss at their child when he indulged in investigative dismemberment of toys. They really lay down the law: "No more of that. Those toys cost good money, so *play* with them." A much happier solution would be to let the child investigate other objects of less value. Provide a box of gadgets that can be dismembered, screw by screw and piece by piece. A broken clock is a gold mine. How about an old radio? Several manufacturers offer very simple motors that can be constructed by a preschool child with some supervision. Many toys are now available with dismemberment in mind; they are designed to be taken apart and put back together.

This preoccupation with how things work is my child's "thing," and we both enjoy some fruits of that interest. There is not a piece of anything, old or new, in the house that he cannot identify. The screw of an unidentified something that has lain on the kitchen window sill for months is no mystery to him. He knows exactly what it came from and whether that particular piece is essential to the function of said object. He is a must to have around on cleaning-out days. He is also able to apply his increasing skills to new and more difficult situations—as my Mr. Fix-it. If you have observed how some mechanical things work, you are then in a position to figure out why it does not work. For some children this could lead to mechanical creativity: "That works this way, but I can see that with a change here and there it could be made so that. . . ." Not only do mechanical toys and gadgets give children a chance to experiment, they also provide children opportunities to make their own "thing." They also prepare children to cope with a gadget-filled world—televisions, cassette recorders, appliances, automobiles, computers.

Art materials are another excellent choice in providing the raw materials with which your child can enjoy hours of pleasure and exercise creative leanings. The most common choices for young children include crayons, tempera paint and brushes, paper and scissors, finger paint, clay, collage material, and later pastels, woodburning equipment, glass paint, etching blocks, and spatter painting equipment. To encourage the use of these materials it is important to react enthusiastically to your child's efforts with them. Be interested and appreciative of what he does. Display pictures and drawings in a special place. Hang them in a desk blotter frame in the kitchen or bedroom for such a display and change the picture frequently—the blotter frame is useful because the pictures can be quickly slipped under the four corners on top of the blotter.

Working with papier-mâché is particularly suited to encouraging creativity. Two methods are described below: one is for pulp-papier-mâché that produces a molded shape and the other, probably better suited to younger children, is strip papier-mâché.

PAPIER-MÂCHÉ (PULP)—Recipe for one cup of pulp: Use three large sheets of newspaper. Tear into small pieces about the size of a dime. (Tear into strips and then tear the strips into dime-sized pieces.) Drop them into warm water and soak for several hours or overnight. Use two smooth sticks, such as old broom handles, to pound and grind paper into pulp. Make the pulp very fine so that no bits of paper can be seen. Place the mixture in an old stocking and squeeze out all excess water. Store in a covered plastic container until ready for use.

PASTE—To be used in both recipes:

Mix together:	two cups flour
	two teaspoons salt or alum
Add gradually:	two cups hot water

Put in pan and boil on stove until clear. Beat until smooth.

Add one part paste to two parts pulp and mix thoroughly. Put in a small plastic bag and squeeze to accomplish the mixing with less mess. Remove from the bag and shape and mold as desired. Allow to dry thoroughly. Paint as desired.

PAPIER-MÂCHÉ (STRIP):

Make paste according to directions in preceding recipe and have ready. Tear large sheets of newspaper into strips and place singly in a large pan of water. While the strips soak, you and your child can locate a bowl or vase around which to shape your papier-mâché object. Lay the bowl, open end down, on a working surface. Apply one strip of paper at a time with paste. Make a single layer, placing one strip at a time across the bowl, pasted side up (away from the bowl). Position each strip so as to completely cover the entire surface of the bowl. Now reverse the process and make a second layer of strips, positioning them with the glue side down. (The reason for the reversal is that you do not want the bottom layer of paper to be pasted to the bowl, since, when all the layers are completed, the bowl inside is removed and the papier-mâché object is left intact.)

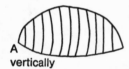
A
vertically

The first layer of strips are placed so that they cover the bowl horizontally. The remaining layers may be placed so that the strips of each layer lie in the same direction, but you change this direction for each successive layer.

B
horizontally

Continue adding layers of paper strips with paste until the object is of desired thickness. Four layers is enough for a beginner's bowl. Carefully remove the papier-mâché object from the mold and allow to dry. To speed the drying process, place on a very lightly greased baking sheet and bake in 250-degree oven for five or ten minutes. When thoroughly dry, paint the creation the color of your choice.

C
diagonally

A great variety of objects are suitable to serve as the base or mold for making a papier-mâché creation. If your child has luck with the bowl and seems to enjoy it, suggest trying some fruit to put in the bowl. After covering the fruit with the paper strips and paste, just as with the bowl, allow them to dry, then split one side with a razor blade far enough to remove the fruit object inside.

criss-cross

74

Mend the slit with paper tape and paint the fruit the appropriate color. Your four-year-old can make a bowl filled with a banana, an apple, and an orange that you and he will be proud to display. Using an artificial green stem and leaf in the apple or orange might add to its attractiveness.

Rainbow Crayons utilizing broken crayons are fun to make and use. To make them, peel the paper off of short, broken, and discardable crayons. Put the pieces in a plastic bag and beat with a hammer, or grate into small pieces on a safety grater. Sprinkle the pieces along the middle of a doubled strip of aluminum wrap. Set the paper in the sun to melt the crayon bits. When they are very soft, roll the paper over to shape the melted bits into one giant crayon. Secure the ends to prevent spilling. Remove from the sun and cool until hardened. Unpeel the aluminum wrap and see what effects your child can achieve with his Rainbow Crayon.

OPEN DOORS

You are now well on your way to seeing possibilities for encouraging creativity everywhere. There are numerous and obvious areas left untouched for you and your child to explore on your own. If you stimulate your child's interest in areas where he already finds pleasure, you will open doors of enjoyment for him that will last a lifetime. If you help your child to explore his talents and to develop his creative skills in whatever area they happen to lie, he will be a more fully developed, a more productive, and a more truly complete individual. As a human being, you want your child's abilities to be developed to the fullest extent for his good and for the good of his world. There are many problems facing our generation and his which cry for creative solutions. Prepare your child to contribute his best by contributing creatively: that is his best.

9 CHAPTER

Muscles and the Mind

The body moves and performs at the mind's command beyond the simple reflex level, yet brain versus brawn — or mental achievement versus physical skill — was a day versus night proposition for earlier thinkers. They assumed that when one existed, the other did not. The muscular body indicated an empty head, and the brain-child was invariably the ninety-pound weakling. Such a hypothesis may have received strength from numerous incidents of compensation — a child experiences failure in one area and leaves off further attempts of that sort, devoting time and energy to developing what he considers to be more obtainable goals. However, increased knowledge and understanding of child development have brought to us the realization that the muscles and the mind are a team, and must develop together from early infancy.

Untrained muscles cannot adequately perform skills. A two-month-old baby sees a rattle near him. He makes gross efforts to make contact, arms wildly swinging, with no control of his hands. At this point, his muscles aren't sufficiently mature for him even to grasp the object. A month later the baby can hold the rattle, but his movement to reach for it is still unskilled. The eye and the hand both work, but it will take much experience and growth for them to work together in the smooth, coordinated fashion required to perform the complicated tasks which lie ahead.

READINESS FOR PHYSICAL ACTIVITIES

Development of physical skills can proceed only as sufficient maturation occurs. It is your responsibility to acquaint yourself with the stages of child development so that you will be an adequate judge of this readiness. Very frustrating experiences take place in the name of love when a parent provides toys or encourages play which the child does not have sufficient physical maturation to cope with—such as a football for Daddy's little man, when the ball is too big and too hard for the small child to manage. Experiencing failure with toys or games that are presented too early not only discourages the child from other attempts of this sort, but also makes a negative contribution to the child's self-image which will reflect itself in cognitive experiences as well.

Control of the body's large muscles occurs first, and the small muscles develop later. Psychologists call this development cephalo-caudal (from head to toe) and proximo-distal (from near to far, trunk–out). Consequently you will notice that your child will develop control and use of his head before such control appears lower in his trunk. Likewise, he will gain earlier management of his larger body movement before he achieves fine control of his extremities and their small muscles. Be closely aware of clues about whether an activity is within the physical reach of your child. A good guide is this: if it is fun for your child, it is appropriate.

A child learns through play. Child's play can be very serious—it can be hard work. It is certainly important. Earlier chapters have outlined how concept development, as well as number and language skills, can be acquired through the medium of play, but the obvious physical play of running, skipping, hopping, and similar overt activities are equally important. You should provide considerable opportunity for such play to ensure the development of your child's physical coordination. During the infant stage he grows at a very rapid rate, and the largest portion of his energy is channeled in this direction—growing. The early movements of lifting his head, and then, later, of crawling and walking, are exercises that strengthen the body muscles and bring him to a stage of readiness for coordinated play.

UNILATERAL DOMINANCE

From birth to twelve months the majority of babies tend to be left handed; however, at about the age of twelve months, a child becomes ambidextrous and remains so until dominance of hand, eye, and foot are definitely established at approximately six and a half years of age. For eighty-five percent of the population, the right side will be the dominant side. In the years between one and six the child will begin to show an increasing preference for one hand or the other. Which side emerges dominant is of little importance. What is important is that your child establish a dominant side and that it be the same for eye, hand, and foot. Be conscious of the side that he chooses naturally, which foot he favors for kicking, or "leading off," which hand he uses for throwing or feeding himself. From that time he should be encouraged to use the preferred hand and foot and establish dominance of one side. Ambidexterity should be discouraged—extensive work in the area of reading disabilities have led some authorities to suspect that such difficulties, as well as stuttering, may be attributable to the absence of consistent dominance. Many of the games outlined in this chapter will provide you with opportunities to encourage your child to use the preferred hand and foot.

As your child develops new skills, such as walking and running, just the act itself will be very pleasurable. If you will simply allow the activity, it will be done. (It may be necessary to make the early distinction that running is for outside, that jumping is fun and is allowed in certain rooms—the idea being that there is a place for each kind of activity and that rules must be established to avoid conflict. Children learn quickly where there is consistency, but they become confused when they are allowed to do one thing today and not tomorrow.)

A stick horse makes running lots of fun, for while your child's muscles are being exercised his imagination is also at work. If you don't already have a horse, you can easily make one. Using a man's old sock, stuff it with crumpled newspaper, old nylon stockings, or any soft material. Use fingers from an old glove for ears. Stuff them and sew them into place. Securely sew on buttons for eyes, or paint a face. Push a broomstick well up into the stuffing and tie the opening securely with a cord. Fasten strips of ribbon or strings to the broomstick for bridle and reins. Galloping is useful for developing a sense of rhythm as well as for providing large-muscle movement. Other imaginative games can provide indoor fun and exercise: how does an elephant walk, a duck waddle, a frog jump, a dog roll over, a kangaroo hop, a kitten climb, a bee buzz, an airplane fly?

A wagon is a very suitable and satisfying toy that promotes physical skills. First the wagon can be pushed, pulled, or climbed into. Later it can be filled with blocks, dolls, or friends, and then pulled or ridden. Other vehicular toys provide good exercise and hours of fun: tricycles, scooters, jeeps that run on a chain drive, and, later, bicycles.

Certain outdoor play equipment is very good and requires only your supervision to be used to advantage. Gym sets, climbing bars, seesaws, trampolines, slides, and merry-go-rounds are the most usual items, but in almost every case you can construct or substitute something that will provide the same exercise if buying the equipment is not feasible, or if you wish to make your own.

One of the most versatile and entertaining things to have around is a strong rope hanging from a tree limb. The rope can be used in many ways. You can tie knots in it at various intervals for climbing; you can hang a tire from it for swinging; you can make a hole in the center of a circular board, pass the rope through the hole, tie a knot underneath and have a great swing; or you can knot the legs of an old pair of blue jeans, fill them with sand, secure the tops, and hang them from the rope to make a great punching bag.

Jumping, which provides for large-muscle development and body coordination, can be encouraged by making a trampoline out of a large truck or tractor inner-tube and a piece of canvas. Cut two circles of canvas as large as the top and bottom of the inflated tube. Make holes around the edges of the canvas with an eyelet punch and reinforce the holes with metal eyelets. Using a strong cord, lace tightly from one canvas to the other as when lacing shoes. This is just the beginning of what you can do with ingenuity, odds and ends, and time.

Balls are popular and appropriate for strengthening arm and back muscles as well as for developing eye-hand coordination. Rolling, kicking, chasing, throwing, and bouncing balls will later lead to games involving higher-level skills.

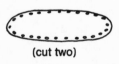

(cut two)

A walking board is good for developing body and foot coordination and a sense of balance. By placing a concrete building block or two bricks under each end of a large board (two-by-six), you will have the necessary apparatus for your child to practice on. Have him walk from end to end. Make up variations for walking forward, sideways, with arms outstretched, hands on hips, with arms folded, walking on tiptoes, following a rhythm forward and then backward, such as *one–two–one/two/three.*

Stilts and tin-can walkers are great for further development or coordination. Stilts have always had a special place in my heart because of a favorite story from my mother's childhood. One of eight children and a preacher's daughter, she moved frequently. Each time her family moved to a new parsonage, the first thing my grandfather did to offer continuity to uprooted lives was to make new stilts for his children. To make them as he did, start with a piece of two-by-four lumber about five feet long. Rip the two-by-four in half lengthwise to make two pieces for uprights. Check the edges for splinters. Using wood scraps, shape two triangular foot pieces. Nail the foot pieces to the two-by-twos so that the top edge of the foot piece is approximately two-thirds the distance from the ground to your child's knee. For older children the foot pieces can be located as high as the knee.

Tin-can walkers are made from large cans (a large juice can or gallon-sized food can). Put the opened edge to the ground and, with the closed end up, make two holes directly across from each other in the side just below the top edge. You can support the cans inside with a wooden block to keep them from bending as you punch the holes. File the rough edges on the inside so they will not cut your string. Now, thread a cord through both holes and tie the ends together, leaving the string long enough so that your child can stand on the cans straight up and still hold the string in his hand. As your child develops skill with these walking toys you might invent a game to see if he can walk in a hop-scotch pattern without losing his balance.

Somewhere in the life of your child skipping, rope-jumping, and skating will appear. These skills are more advanced and should not be encouraged until your child definitely shows readiness for them. However, when he does, they will prove to be very good activities for refining body coordination. For a child who has difficulty jumping rope, try singing a song with a good rhythm. It will help him keep a beat for jumping. After this skill is mastered, you might suggest some variations such as jumping on one foot and then the other, jumping into a turning rope, jumping five times and then out, jumping in and asking a friend to jump in beside him, jumping out together when the song or rhyme is over.

Another variation of rope-jumping requires tying a weight, such as a beanbag, to the end of a three- or four-foot rope. Stoop or kneel on the ground, and, alternating from hand to hand, smoothly swing the rope around you in a circle. Keep it close to the ground or floor. Direct your child to watch it carefully and jump over as the rope approaches him. Several children playing this together have even more fun.

As you are considering games and play equipment to promote physical coordination and development, don't overlook the obvious opportunities in daily living. If you usually drive everywhere, leave the car at home occasionally and walk, skip, hop, run, and jump on a short errand with your child. Let him help you in gardening and yard work. While you weed, let him have a shovel to dig. While you cut the grass, let him pick up sticks or rake at a safe distance. While edging, let him sweep the walk and the steps. If you live in an apartment or have no yard, let your child help you sort laundry, set the table, or assist you in other chores. There are extra dividends here beside the physical skills you are promoting: the age of three is not too early to begin assuming some responsibility for small chores, and working with you is the best way to begin. Not only is it more fun, but you show him by your example how to stick with a job until it is completed.

As the large muscles develop and become controlled, it is time to introduce or encourage games which promote small muscle development. Before considering specific activities in this category, I would like to mention that visual skills are an intricate part of motor development. The activities for which you are preparing your child, such as reading, writing, and number work, require the eyes to work with the hands. Almost any manual skill has a visual element, so we speak of visual-motor activities. As you include games for small-muscle development, be aware of the added dimension of visual skills.

Earliest activities for developing small muscles are largely manipulative: cutting, pasting, coloring, painting, block building, working puzzles, and modeling in clay. Many commercial clays are available, of both water and oil base, but homemade clay-dough is very satisfying and can be made in the color of your choice. An easy recipe that makes a good-size ball requires:

> two cups flour
> one cup salt
> one to two tablespoons of cooking oil
> water
> a few drops of food coloring

Mix the dry ingredients, add oil slowly, then water a little at a time until the dough becomes pliable and holds together. If it is too stiff, add more water; if it is too sticky, add more salt. Since small-muscle exercise is your aim, leave it as stiff as possible. Color it any color you like. To preserve it, seal it in a plastic container— it won't keep indefinitely, but it will remain satisfactory for several weeks, and then a fresh batch will be in order. Kneading, shaping, and rolling the clay is very good for small muscle development.

Your child might enjoy using a rolling pin and cookie cutter to make Christmas tree ornaments from the homemade clay-dough. After rolling and cutting them, use a straw to make a hole in the top of each shape. Bake in a 300-degree oven on a cookie sheet for an hour to harden. Dry overnight and paint them if you wish. Hang them with ribbons strung through the hole. If your child molds something that he likes particularly well, you can bake it as you do the cookie shapes to preserve it for him. He can also use the shapes for play jewelry, tying a ribbon through the hole and wearing one piece as a necklace after baking and painting it. However, my experience is that children find the most fun in shaping and changing, not saving.

CUTTING AND PASTING

Using scissors is another very good activity for the development of small muscles. Many parents refuse to let little children handle scissors, or else they give them very inexpensive ones that are quite hard to use, but a three-year-old child can use appropriate scissors safely with supervision. So, spend a little more and buy a good pair of children's scissors, see that they do cut and operate efficiently, and plan for time to oversee the activity.

Cutting newspapers, pictures from old magazines, or strips of construction paper for making paper chains are good experiences for your child before he can exercise sufficient control to actually cut carefully "along the lines." Let pleasure and practice be your aim for him, rather than a perfectly done job. If he likes to cut and paste, you may wish to teach him to make his own paste from flour and water. Any mixing activity is good exercise for fingers.

COLORING AND PAINTING

Crayons are universal favorites, and you should introduce them early. Purchase crayons which are large in diameter—small hands can control and use a larger crayon more easily than a smaller one. A box of seven is plenty in the beginning; wait until your child is older to experiment with a box of fifty-four different colors. If you want to provide a big box of something, make it a big box of paper—*big* paper. Initial coloring efforts will use more large muscles than small ones and arm motion requires a good-sized piece of paper. A pack of newsprint is a very good investment. A friend and former kindergarten teacher advocates using the back side of junk mail for drawing and coloring paper. When her school was pinching pennies, she kept her pupils in paper this way. It's not just in the interests of conservation that I mention this; I truly think it's more fun for you and your child to cultivate the ability to utilize scrap materials for pleasure than to know only how to enjoy and use things you buy. Keep a good sturdy box (perhaps an old stationery or dress box) for the paper, scissors, crayons, and paste. Let cleaning up and putting away be part of the activity.

Coloring books are fine, but don't use them exclusively and don't expect neat pictures from early efforts. If your child always prefers a coloring book to a blank piece of paper and crayons, it may be because you haven't provided sufficient opportunity for creative work or an environment of acceptance for the finished product. It is encouraging for a child to see his work displayed, and admiring comments from the ones who love him motivate him to continuing efforts.

For a slightly older child who can manage a brush without frustrating accidents, painting is a worthwhile activity, but we don't always make paint and water available to our children. The kitchen table is usually a pretty safe place to paint, but if you object so much to the mess made that you always have a reason for why it is not a good time to paint, try setting up a small table outside on pretty days. Better still, make an easel and use it often outdoors. To make it, use a large cardboard box from which you remove two opposite sides leaving the remaining two opposing sides and bottom intact. Remove the flaps from the sides if there are any. Bring the two sides together at the top and secure with holes with string or tape. Your easel now has a triangular shape.

Paper for painting can now be attached to either side

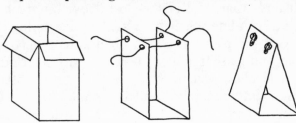

of the easel with thumb tacks, or more permanent fasteners could be fashioned by fastening two clothes-pins (one in each top corner) for holding the paper. To secure the clothespin to the easel, punch a small hole in the box on either side of the spot where you wish to locate the clothespin. Push a string through the holes over and under the clothespin at the joint until it is securely fastened.

Besides water color and tempera painting, finger painting is very satisfying to a child and provides variety and slightly different muscular activity. Finger paint goes very quickly, so you might like to know how to make your own.

> Soften two cups of Argo starch in a small amount of cold water.
> Stir.
> Add this to one quart of boiling water.
> Make thick starch by stirring until the mixture bubbles.
> Remove from stove and cool.
> Add one half cup Ivory Soap Flakes (do not substitute).
> Store in a covered jar in a cool place, until ready for use.
> Then divide into several small plastic containers and color each with a different food color. A muffin tin can be used in the absence of suitable jars.

Your child may need more help than usual from you in learning to use this material, so plan to do a few pictures with him, showing him how to place an adequate amount of paint on the paper and then to use his fingers, arms, and elbows to achieve different effects. String a line somewhere to allow for drying and displaying the pictures; if your child is unusually productive, and space is limited, a portable wooden clothes dryer will allow you to dry several pictures without making a clutter on every available counter top. Set the dryer in the bathtub if you have no other available place where dripped paint can be removed easily.

If you have a handyman in your family, there will be some wonderful equipment a child can learn to use: scraps of wood, nails, saws for cutting, and a hammer. Just driving nails into wood is sufficient at first. Later, simple construction will be possible. A boat or a car can be very rough and still be an object of pride. You might save empty spools, small wooden boxes, and other throwaway items in a scrap box to be brought out on a special day when supervision of such an activity is possible. You are not always in the mood to be a cheerful companion to a four-year-old handyman, so keep the material available for the right time.

USING A PENCIL

Children love to trace things. This pursuit helps to develop control of the small muscles in the hands as well as stimulate eye-hand coordination. Can the hand do what the mind directs and the eyes see? With your child, make a collection of small objects that your child can trace around, such as bottle and jar lids, cookie cutters, small boxes, or pieces of jewelry. Paper and pencil are the only additional things you need. Tracing around and then looking at the resulting design is good four-year-old fun.

As your child begins to handle and use a pencil, it would be well to see that he is holding it correctly in his fingers. Once a child has become accustomed to holding a pencil incorrectly, it is difficult to effect a change to the correct position.

SHOE-LACING

Another absorbing activity for finger and eye that will make you very popular with your child's first teachers—as well as with your child—is lacing shoes. Several lacing devices are available from well-known toy manufacturers, but you can make one easily. Make a big shoe out of a cardboard box, using any side that is intact.

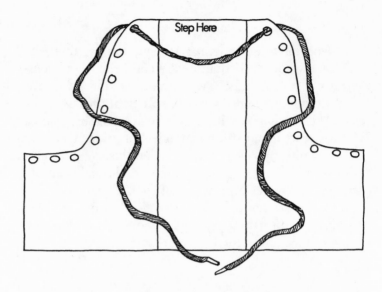

Punch holes at least one half inch in diameter along both edges. Fold the shoe so that the center section is flat on the floor. Help your child put his foot on the flat surface so that the sides of the shoe fold against both sides of his ankle. Use a long lace or large cotton cord with tape around each end to make a stiff end for lacing. Now show your child how and let him practice lacing and unlacing the shoe. Later he will be ready for tying the bow.

GROUP ACTIVITIES

If you implement these suggestions to ensure development of your child's physical coordination, you may well attract a crowd in neighborhoods where young children come from a few houses away to play, or when your friends bring their children over. The games and activities I have already mentioned lend themselves well to entertaining several children, but there is another group of visual-motor games that should be especially popular with groups of preschool or slightly older children. Make bowling pins by saving empty plastic jars or bottles and filling them with sand. When you collect a set of six you can make a bowling game. Provide a rubber ball that is large enough for small hands to hold. For three-year-olds a ball about six or eight inches in diameter is fine. For four- and five-year-olds, almost any average rubber ball will do. Make a pattern for the pin setter on a large grocery bag, opened at the seam. Mark the correct position for the pins on the bag.

The children then take turns being the bowler and the pin setter. If scorekeeping appeals to them, but they don't write numerals yet, show them how to tally and then count the tally marks. Score one for each pin knocked down. You might want to add a bonus for a strike or a spare. If you don't happen to have a ball handy, or if you want to introduce a little variety, a beanbag can be thrown at the pins. Of course you will need to limit this game to an area where the beanbag can be thrown safely.

A beanbag with its own special target box is another wonderful and entertaining game to develop eye-hand coordination. For three-, four-, and five-year-olds, a bag about three inches by four inches made from sturdy scraps of material and filled with rice or dried peas is very good. Beanbags can be made in many clever shapes, but I believe the extra effort would be more appreciated by an older child. The preschooler just wants a chance to *throw*. Save a cardboard box with sides at least twelve inches deep. This dimension will give the box more stability when it becomes a target. Draw a good sassy face on the box, making holes in the position of eyes, nose, and mouth. The holes should be twice as large as the beanbag for a beginner at this game. Set the box at a suitable distance for a target and

weight it with a brick or books to hold it steady. Now just stand back and watch the bags fly. This is another game in which tally scoring can be used to reinforce number concepts. Count one for a mouth hit (the largest opening), two for a hit in the eye hole, and three for a hit through the nose (which should be the smallest hole). Not only do these target games develop good eye-hand coordination, they also provide a satisfying and acceptable outlet for aggressive feelings.

Playing with the beanbag alone may be the preference of your child. If there are several small children in your family or neighborhood, make several bags instead of one. They can play hot potato, tossing the beanbag back and forth until a phonograph record stops, or simply have fun tossing and catching.

Another exhilarating game is keeping a balloon in the air for as long as possible by throwing it up and hitting it back each time with their hands as soon as it comes into range. This is excellent preparation for any sport or activity in which keeping the eyes on a moving object is important.

EMOTIONAL READINESS FOR PHYSICAL ACTIVITIES

Function of mind, muscles, and emotions are inseparable. The mind commands and the muscles respond—but only to do those things which a person is emotionally prepared to accomplish. An incident during my young son's swimming lessons illustrated this point clearly to me. Shortly after he learned to stay afloat, his swimming instructor told him to dive off the board. He got into diving position but could not make himself jump. The next day he asked me to take him swimming, saying that he wanted to learn to jump off the board. After swimming for a while he wanted to slide down the ladder chute into the water, with the understanding that I would catch him when he surfaced. After sliding down a few times and getting out of the water with my assistance, he asked me to let him swim to the side of the pool by himself. After he had done this two or three times, he turned to me and said, "Now I want to jump off of the diving board." When we approached the board he said to me, "You stay out of the water; I can do it alone." His muscles had been capable of diving and swimming for several days, his mind told his muscles to act at his instructor's original command to dive, but he did not possess the emotional security for diving until he was sure he had mastered the prerequisite skills.

Readiness skills are important for continuing physical and mental achievement, but emotional security is equally important. The physically awkward child and the mentally awkward child usually acquire a poor self-image. A child who views himself poorly in relation to others often does poorly in school. Through awareness, planning, encouraging, and implementing suitable activities, you can help your child to develop both his muscles and his mind.

CHAPTER

Just for Fun

Just for fun means exactly that—it means not trying to accomplish or to advance or to expand anything, but just to enjoy. It is most desirable to enjoy being with your child and he with you, having no end in mind other than experiencing the simple, warm, genuine pleasure of being in each other's company.

Very quickly and of necessity children become engrossed in the business of life, as Whittier recalled in "The Barefoot Boy":

> All too soon these feet must hide
> In the prison cells of pride,
> Lose the freedom of the sod,
> Like a colt's for work be shod,
>
> • • •
>
> Cheerily then, my little man—
> Live and laugh as boyhood can.

In this relatively carefree time of early childhood, you

have an opportunity to set a pattern for pleasure with your children. If you don't do it then, the chances are good that you can't do it at all. You may learn to enjoy them later, but they probably won't learn to enjoy you.

You can and should capitalize on the medium of play to teach your child, but learning should be accomplished not only through the medium of play, but also in the spirit of play. When playing a developmental game with your child, don't pressure him to conform to certain standards you have arbitrarily set, and avoid a drill-type atmosphere or an attitude of disappointment if results do not measure up to expectations. You can guide your child and give some direction to his play without robbing him of its pleasure.

There should, however, be opportunities in daily life for you to have *fun* together with your child—not "run outside and play" time, which is good and much a part of a child's day, but time "we" spend together in quiet or noisy, strenuous or restful, productive or more passive pursuits.

I recently asked a four-year-old what she did with her mother or daddy that was the very most fun. She answered after some serious thought, "Hug them." Your activity does not have to be highly structured to be the highlight of your child's day. In fact, as structure decreases, the quality and value of playtime together probably increases, because you will be filling in the gap with more of yourself, which is a decided asset.

What would your child answer if he were asked what he liked to do best with you? To some little boys it might be having thirty minutes of Daddy's time to pitch a ball back and forth, or it might be walking around the block together—this time not to "learn to see" but to learn and have fun together.

The mother of the four-year-old mentioned above assured herself and her three children of the opportunity to enjoy a strictly fun time by planning for it. As her children grew beyond the infant stage and they began to compete increasingly for their parents' time and attention, she hit upon a happy solution: thirty minutes for each child sometime during the day—a special time to be used as each child chose. For this special time, his parent's time and attention was completely his. Sometimes they might go outdoors to walk or play; sometimes they might play a game indoors or work on a construction project together, and sometimes they might just sit and read books—side by side.

Such just-for-fun time is very valuable. Helping your child is important, not serious; and having fun is pleasant, not frivolous. Taking ourselves too seriously is a terrible mistake, so save some time for fun, and cultivate an atmosphere that promotes fun. Doing the dishes with my mother was fun, because she knew how to make it so. Do some homework at your house. Set a time for nonsense and see what develops. What would your child enjoy doing with you? By calling it nonsense, you may find out. He'll know that nonsense can include anything!

You will want to vary times of quiet companionship with other kinds of fun, but keep in mind that a good balance between the two will enhance the pleasure derived from each.

Here are some additional prescriptions for fun—take one regularly to promote good family health. If you do so, and find that your child learns something in the process, great! No matter what a child is doing, he is learning something.

PLAY FURNITURE

Play furniture is equally as entertaining to make as it is to use. Obtain several large cardboard boxes, such as packing boxes from refrigerators, stoves, and TV appliances. The latter are excellent because some of them are reinforced inside with wood. These are in good supply before Christmas when large orders of merchandise are arriving in the stores. Check at a store where you have done business. A good box is important.

Play stove: To make a stove, use one rather square box. Improvise a raised back (about six inches high) as

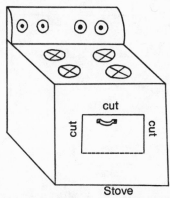

Stove

a panel for the stove dials. If you have an appliance packing box there are usually some blocks of styrofoam inside used in packaging and bracing the appliance. These are perfect. Glue the styrofoam blocks to the back of the stove top. Cover four bottle caps with aluminum foil, hammer a hole in the center of each, and attach to the styrofoam panel at spaced intervals with nails. Position burners on the top surface by cutting holes as large as the bottom of small disposable aluminum pans (like pot-pie pans). The fluted rim of the pans will keep them from falling through the holes. Cross popsicle sticks and extend the ends into opposite sides of the pie pans to make a rack for holding the cooking implements. Cut the oven door on three sides, leaving the bottom side connected to the stove box. Fashion a handle on the stove door (aluminum strip secured with paper brads) so the door can be opened and closed. Make at least one shelf inside the oven for cooking. To do so, cut a piece of cardboard four inches wider than you want the shelf. Bend down a strip two inches wide on opposite sides of the cardboard piece and place these two inch folded sides flat against the opposite sides of the interior of the oven. Either staple or use paper brads through both thicknesses (shelf and stove side) to secure the shelf to the stove. Make oven controls of covered bottle caps and secure to the face of the stove box above the oven door. Cover the entire appliance with shelf paper or paint.

Play sink: Use the same type box as was used for the

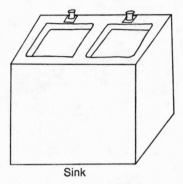

Sink

stove. Make a single- or double-bowl sink by cutting holes in the top of the box the size of an available plastic dish which has a rim at the edge. The rim of the bowl will keep it from falling through the hole. It is better to cut the hole a little too small to begin since you can always make it larger if necessary. Set the dish or dishes in the holes. If you make a single-bowl sink, it can be round. Position it to one side or the other to leave some working space, perhaps for a play dish drainer. For faucets use large empty thread spools. Nail the spools to small blocks of wood or styrofoam leaving the spools loose enough to turn. Glue the wood or styrofoam blocks to the sink in the proper location. Paint or cover the sink as you did the stove. Your sink will hold water, which adds greatly to the fun.

Play cupboard: Use two boxes, exactly the same size if possible. One will be the bottom of the cupboard. Cut two doors as illustrated and attach handles. Make a shelf or shelves inside using the method described in making shelves for the play stove. Cut the second box so that it is exactly half as tall as the bottom. Set the smaller box on its side on the top of the cupboard base (see illustration). Use a strip of the cardboard you cut off to make a shelf in the top half of the cupboard. Cover or paint the cupboard as the other pieces.

Play refrigerator: For this appliance you will need a large, tall box. Cut a small door in the top portion for the freezer and, leaving a strip in between for stability, cut a larger opening in the bottom portion for the refrig-

96

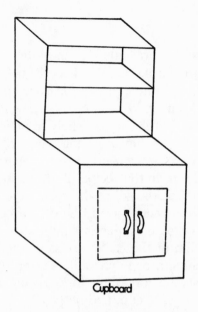

Cupboard

erator door. Position shelves in both sections using techniques suggested earlier. In the bottom of the refrigerator, set two smaller boxes side by side to be the hydrators—one for fruits and one for vegetables. If necessary, place them on the bottom shelf so they can be slipped in and out with ease. Paint or cover the refrigerator to match the other appliances in the kitchen.

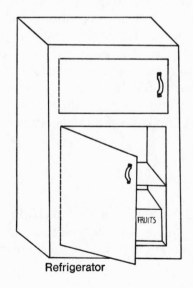

FRUITS

Refrigerator

"Cook Wanted"

Imaginative play with food and kitchen equipment is fun, but preparing real food for actual meals is even better. Plan a simple meal with your child including a dish that your child can prepare. Beginning at lunch might be easiest if you are likely to be less pressed for time at the noon hour. Decide who will do what. Cut pictures from a magazine to represent the ingredients your child uses in the recipe. Paste them in a notebook to make a "cookbook" of the recipes you try together. The different recipes could be organized into sections of meats, vegetables, desserts, and salads, or you could include them in the cookbook as you learn to prepare them. Include a page on table setting, illustrating the correct location for knife, fork, spoon, napkin, plate, salad bowl, glass, cup, and saucer.

"What's for Lunch, Bunch?"

This game is fun for children of varying ages. Cut food pictures from magazines—as many as possible of foods of every kind: bread, pies, meat, fruit, vegetable dishes, drinks, and snacks. Stack or arrange the pictures in a place convenient to the "waiter." Customers sit at a card table set with paper plates and order any food their hearts desire. The waiter uses his pad to record the selections (he will probably have to draw clues for himself to remember the order). He then proceeds to the kitchen to fill the order. He "serves up" with a flourish the pictures representing each order and the customers let him know if he remembered it accurately.

"It's My Town"

This game is nice for parent and child alone or with a small group. Make a town. Select an area where an activity can remain in place for several days. Use strips of paper at least six inches wide for the streets. Place them at right angles. Use paper milk cartons for buildings. Half-pint milk containers are good for houses and the quart or half-gallon size make skyscrapers when upright, and apartments and municipal buildings when placed on their side. Cover the cartons with construction paper and decorate with crayons or magic markers. Make signs for your buildings by taping and

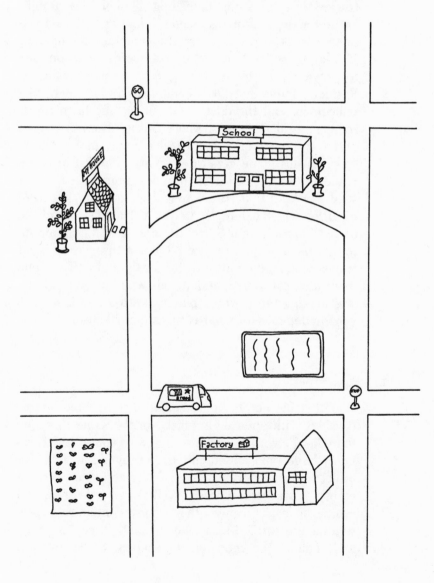

labeling either end of rectangular paper signs to tooth-picks and stick in the top of the buildings to identify them. Make traffic signs of popsicle sticks or lead pencils; stick them in a small ball of clay to stand them up and glue the sign you have made of construction paper to the top.

When the toy cars and trucks begin to roll the traffic signs can be changed to direct the traffic. Mark the trucks with some distinguishing symbol like a milk bottle for the milkman's wagon, a loaf of bread on the bakery truck, a piece of furniture for the moving van. If small dolls are handy they could ride in or on cars to provide your town with some community helpers. Fashion simple hats to distinguish the fireman, the policeman, and the doctor. Of course, the town needs some natural resources. Make bushes from crumpled green crepe paper—or stick live twigs in an empty spool. If this game generates enough interest to last a while, put some rich dirt in a small aluminum pan, plant seeds—a kind that sprout quickly—and you will have a garden which can be located in a strategic spot in the town. Want a beach? Sprinkle some sand on aluminum foil. Want a swimming pool? Paint a throwaway meat tray blue and add a little water for the right effect. The town idea can be expanded, but whether you emphasize making the town or playing with a less elaborate version depends on what is fun at your house.

"LET'S PLAY STORE"

With some empty boxes set up a store. Stack boxes on sides with open ends turned in the same direction to make shelves for groceries. Rig up a counter by turning a large box, closed-end up, or by using a bridge table. Collect empty cans (check for any sharp edges), empty plastic containers with labels, empty cereal and cookie boxes, and any other empty containers representing groceries. Make play money. Price the stock and organize the goods on the shelves. Use a toy cash register or improvise one by sectioning a cigar box. The "customer" will need a basket to collect his selection of groceries and the "grocer" may need a pad to figure the bill.

Not all of your child's playtime will be spent at home. The family vacation, or any trip, may mean long hours of traveling that can be very boring to a young child. Parents don't enjoy traveling with a restless youngster either. Some of the problems can be solved by advance planning and ingenuity on the parent's part, turning this time into a marvelous opportunity for games and fun. A box or bag of paper and crayons, a special picture book, possibly connected with the area to which you are traveling, a deck of cards, a sticker book, are all good basic equipment. A trip to the dime store for a few new coloring- or sticker-books before the trip will provide you with some surprise treats. Perhaps you should keep them hidden under the seat as emergency supplies.

The passing scenery provides opportunities for games that can't be played at home. Old favorites like Cow Poker still delight and entertain children. Each player chooses a side of the car and, beginning at the same time, the players count all four-legged animals they see on their respective sides. If you pass a cemetery you lose your count and have to start over, but only if it is on your side. The first one to reach one hundred wins. If your child is too small to count to one hundred, adjust to his level, make it ten or twenty-five.

If you are traveling in a section of the country where animals are not readily visible, choose something else to count, perhaps all things of a particular color.

Another game for somewhat older children that utilizes passing scenery and signs is Alphabet Poker. Again, choose sides of the car from which to look. The object is to find the letters of the alphabet in consecutive

101

order on signs, billboards, or anything else that you pass on your side. Road signs, billboards, store signs, mailboxes—any written letters are acceptable. Be sure to "play" aloud as this increases the competitive spirit and the fun.

Guessing games provide a change of pace when scenery has lost its appeal. Who Am I, one of the oldest games I know, is still good. One person is "it" and thinks of a person known to everyone playing. The players in turn ask one question, to be answered yes or no, in an attempt to guess the identity of the person that "it" has chosen. Very young children will immediately begin by guessing names of individuals. It is interesting to play with them and observe the way their style of playing will change. As you ask questions that narrow the possibilities rather than guessing specific people, the children will gradually learn from you. Soon they will be following your example and will ask more efficient questions such as "Are you a girl?" "Do you live in my block?" "Do you go to my school?" instead of beginning with "Are you Tom?" "Are you my mother?" "Are you my friend, Jim?"

Another simple guessing game that very small children can play, but older ones enjoy as well, is I See ——— (a color). You are limited in your choice to the inside of the car. The player who is "it" looks around the inside of the car and selects an object. He identifies only its color by declaring, "I see something red." The players in turn try to guess what the object is. The one who guesses correctly is then "it."

In this ecology-conscious era you can make a game of keeping your car interior, and the road along which you are passing, clean and neat. Provide some kind of receptacle for each person's equipment, as simple as a paper sack, as elaborate as a small flight bag or zippered case. As soon as a game requiring some equipment is finished, pack it away before starting something else. If you have a snack bag, also have a place for the used papers and trash. Take turns being the overseer with authority to point out mess or untended play material.

102

Is there any better time for fun than a birthday? You and your child can extend the pleasure of the day by deciding on a party theme and developing the idea together with lots of ingenuity. Some suggestions are partially developed below—largely to get *your* thinking started. What you and your child come up with will be more fun for you.

Hobo party: Use squares of colorful, printed material to fashion a knapsack. Tie opposite corners of the square cloth together. Secure the knot of the knapsack to the end of a sturdy stick with a string or rubber band. A stick with a natural fork in the end is quite good. (This will help to hold the sack in place securely.) Write a poem or invitation on a torn piece of brown paper bag and pin to the outside of the knapsack—something to this effect:

HOBOS WANTED!
Tuesday, January 12
4:00–6:00
1504 Martin Drive

Bring your knapsack along
for free handout

NO DUDES ALLOWED!

Deliver the knapsacks to the house of each child you plan to invite. If the children live at too great a distance to make this idea practical, you can use the knapsacks for serving refreshments at party time. Perhaps you could have them sticking in a bush or tree near your playing area for decoration until time to eat. In this case, you could send an invitation through the mail—perhaps a hot dog in a bun. Naturally, you would serve hot dogs to your hobos. To make the invitation, cut a bun from light construction paper (white or cream). Edge with a brown crayon or magic marker. Cut the hot dog out of rust or orange construction paper. Write invitation information around the outside edge of the bun and finish up on the hot dog. Fold bun on fold line, slip

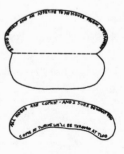

the hot dog inside and mail in a plain envelope to your guests. Plan the party games to carry through the hobo theme. After the guests arrive (if you did deliver the knapsacks) collect them and fill them with a picnic lunch. You could have these prepared and packed in individual paper bags, ready to slip into the knapsack. Give one to each child and hike to a nearby park or playground to eat the lunch and play on the available play equipment. Everyone keeps his knapsack as a party souvenir: you might include a small favor inside, like ball and jacks, or a sack of marbles.

Pirate party: Send your invitations out on a skull and crossbones made of construction paper. As the guests arrive, present each with a pirate patch you have prepared in advance. For this use a scrap of material large enough to cover a child's eye; tape it over a ten-inch length of elastic string tied at the ends. Have paper ready for guests to make and decorate their own pirate hats. Use large pieces of newspaper or shelf paper cut into eighteen-inch squares. Provide tape, paper brads, crayons, or magic markers and help. Be prepared to suggest the following method if guests want assistance. Fold paper diagonally. Bring corners A and B to meet at point C. There are two pieces of paper at point C (formed by folding the square of paper in half in step 1). Fold one "C" end over and over as the fold lines illustrate. This folding will necessitate folding A and B up too. Turn hat over and fold other "C" end up on the fold lines. Secure folded edges with tape or staples.

With hats and patches properly donned, hunt for hidden treasure. Paint an assortment of rocks with gold spray paint or wrap in aluminum foil. Hide the rocks in specified areas of your yard or house before the children arrive. Give each child a sack for his collection and award a prize for the most gold nuggets after the treasure hunt is over. You might have a special prize for whoever finds the Treasure Chest, an appropriately decorated cigar box with gum or candy inside. Arrange with an older neighborhood child or relative to arrive at a strategic time in pirate costume—black pants, black

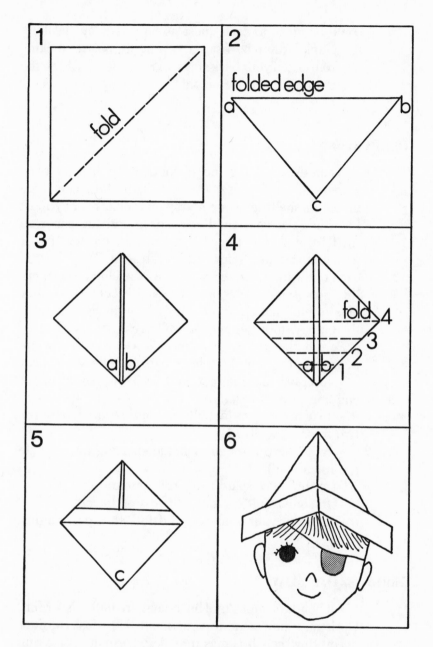

shirt, boots, and eye patch. While your pirate tells a spooky story, you will be relieved to prepare refreshments. Serve from a trunk or foot locker if the refreshment selection permits. If your party budget hasn't been exhausted, rubber swords or other small party favors could be given to each guest as he leaves by "walking the plank," jumping from a two-by-six board, sticking out from one of your back steps, to the ground. Check the height to see if this idea is safe.

ODDS AND ENDS

As an extra party game, or for a time when the gang gathers at your house, this activity is fun. Use large pieces of shelf paper or newspaper sheets. They must be as large as your child or children. Put the paper on the floor and have the children each lie on their paper with arms by their sides and legs straight. Trace around each one with a dark crayon. Now the children can cut themselves out, color and dress the cutouts as they please, and make a most unusual mural by taping all the cutouts to a designated wall area.

For another extra, play Obstacle Course Follow-the-Leader. Set up an obstacle course. Include something:

—to crawl through (cardboard boxes open at either end and pushed together).

—to walk under (a pole or rope secured between two trees.

—to squeeze through (a ladder leaning at an angle against a wall).

—to step into (spare tires, rope circle).

—to somersault on (old mattress or towel).

Check out your house or yard for other possibilities.

HOLIDAYS—HAPPY DAYS

All holidays, much like birthdays, are naturals for fun. Christmas may come to your mind first—just consider decorating the Christmas tree. A suggestion for making Christmas tree ornaments of clay-dough was given in an earlier chapter. It's hard to beat popping popcorn and making strings of leftover corn to trim the tree. An even more decorative string can be made by alternating popcorn with cranberries.

Have you ever tried popcorn balls? You may not want to spare them for the tree, but here's a good recipe:

Pop the amount of popcorn desired (½ cup popped corn per ball).

Salt lightly and cover to tenderize while preparing syrup.

SYRUP: 1/2 cup sugar
      1 cup corn syrup (or white or maple)
      1 tablespoon cider vinegar
      1 tablespoon butter

Directions: Boil first three ingredients until hardball stage is reached. (Drop in cold water to determine if brittle.) Pour one-third of syrup over popcorn, stirring and mixing as you pour. Keep remainder of syrup warm by placing in a pan of hot water—double-boiler fashion. Coat hands with butter, then shape popcorn into balls. The syrup recipe will work up approximately one quart of popcorn; however, it is better to have too much ready than too little. If there is any delay in using the cooked syrup, keep it warm. A neighbor of mine makes these every Christmastime with any children who happen to be handy, but they never decorate the tree!

If you prefer to eat the popcorn balls, another type of ball ornament that is attractive and fun to make together is an Embroidery Floss Balloon Ball. They aren't nearly as hard to make as they are to pronounce, so don't let the title discourage you. You will need packages of embroidery floss in bright colors, some small balloons, some liquid starch, and some glitter. To make: unwrap the floss and place in full-strength liquid-starch concentrate of any brand. When the floss is completely wet, remove it from starch and begin wrapping in a single thread around a balloon blown up to the size of the desired ornament. Wrap in every direction as if you were winding a ball of yarn. The wet floss is likely to tangle. If you have this difficulty, try cutting the package of floss into shorter, more manageable lengths before putting in starch. Don't wind floss around the balloon until it is completely covered; you want some open spaces. After winding, sprinkle glitter lightly over the wet floss. Hang the balloon up to dry (by tying a string from the balloon knot to a coat hanger). When the floss is completely dry, pop the balloon and remove from the center leaving the ornament which is ready to hang on the tree.

Christmas is festive and fun to enjoy with your child, but so are the other holidays—Valentine's Day, Easter, Fourth of July. Fun is really where you learn to find it; with luck you and your child will learn to find it easily and often—together.

School at Last

If you look forward eagerly to your child's first day in school, your child will do likewise. If you have a positive attitude toward school, your child is likely to have a positive attitude. If you feel that people are not trustworthy, if you view teachers and school officials as untrustworthy individuals, school will be a miserable place for your child during twelve years of his life. But if you love learning, if you trust people, and believe that the making of a better world begins with you and your child, your attitude will make school a great place for your child.

P.T.A.ERS

It would be folly for me to imply that Parent-Teacher Associations ever did much for parents. Generally they are low-key organizations with unimaginative programs, but as a former teacher and principal I must reveal that I have never known the child of a parent who attended P.T.A. regularly to have severe problems at school. I do not wish to imply that children of P.T.A.ers are always rapid learners, although many are; but parents who attend P.T.A. regularly exhibit a certain positive attitude which permits them to communicate with school officials, to accept the potentials and limitations of their children, and to build upon what exists. In other words, P.T.A. is not the important variable. The important variable is the attitude exhibited by parents who attend P.T.A.

SCHOOLS ARE NOT GOOD ENOUGH

Neither do I wish to mislead you into thinking that all schools are perfect and should be supported without reservation. To the contrary, I strongly believe that most schools are inadequate, inefficient, and relatively inhumane. I believe that education at all levels can and should be better—much better. But I also believe that we all have a responsibility for making it better. Parents of school children have an obligation to keep abreast of the current thinking and trends in education. They should know the characteristics of good schools and should let school officials know the kind of educational programs they want for their children. Most parents are not educational experts and should never assume that they are, but by knowing the characteristics of good and bad schools they can offer suggestions and encouragement for change and provide support when change comes.

HUMANENESS

Let me enlarge a bit upon what may be found in school when your child finally enrolls. When I refer to schools as being inhumane, I mean that children are not generally permitted to act naturally, or the way humans

110

normally act. At home your child has much freedom of movement. He can talk when he has something to say. He asks questions when his curiosity is aroused, and he changes from one activity to another when he is tired or bored.

Many schools will not permit this kind of behavior. When a child enters first grade he is often required to sit in a chair in a particular row until told to move, remain silent until told to speak, appear interested in what he already knows or something he has no background for learning, work on a given task for a predetermined period of time, and use the bathroom only at prescribed intervals. This kind of activity is not education. This kind of training develops dependence instead of self-initiative. It causes a dislike for school and education rather than a love for learning, and it almost completely stifles creativity.

The above is not meant as condemnation of teachers and school administrators. Most teachers were taught and treated in a similar way at school — as you yourself may have been. Their teacher preparation in colleges reinforced what they had experienced in earlier years. How can they be expected to act differently now? It may take several generations to bring about the needed changes in education throughout the nation. But changes are taking place in many schools now.

New School Trends

Some teachers and school officials are providing a different learning environment. They are making school experiences attractive and enjoyable. They permit children to act like people, and children respond by accepting responsibility, by achieving well, and most importantly, by feeling good about themselves.

I visited a school recently in which five-, six-, and seven-year-old children were acting in a very unusual manner. There were no designated reading, arithmetic, or science periods. Children worked on reading when they chose to do so. As a matter of fact, a child could work on reading for one or two whole days without stopping if that was what he desired to do. Of course, if this behavior continued to the complete neglect of other subjects, he would be redirected. It is seldom that children require extreme redirection. The children in this school could talk when they needed to talk; they could work together and discuss their work without being accused of cheating; they could leave the room when necessity dictated, and they could even take a "coffee break" when tired. A coffee break for these children consisted of playing with blocks and toys for a short time in an inconspicuous corner of the room. When the teacher left the room there was no noticeable change in the behavior of the children. They knew what they were supposed to be learning; they were trusted, and they pursued their tasks with obvious pleasure and determination. How great it is for children to have the opportunity to behave naturally at school!

More and more schools are moving toward a relaxed type of environment and individualized programs. There are numerous models in different parts of the nation worthy of emulation. But in far too many school systems there is insufficient money for teachers and administrators to travel for observation purposes or to employ consultants who can come to them and who can provide the needed direction and impetus for change. But perhaps the greatest single cause of limited progress in educational reform is lack of creativity on the part of educators; a lack brought about by a structure which gives priority to conformity. After years of conforming it is not easy to be innovative. After years of experience in a static environment, it is difficult to change. But changes are being made.

The chances are excellent that your child will enroll in a fine school and have experiences with wonderful teachers, for there are many good elementary schools today, and the good ones are becoming more numerous. This individualization is made possible, in part, because school staffs are beginning to define more precisely and scientifically the skills that a child must learn, and are taking into account a child's previously acquired skills and concepts. When a child's educational program is so exactly charted, it becomes possible to use all kinds of instructional media, including computers, in its fulfillment. It is exciting to anticipate what lies ahead in education, and to know that you can influence its direction. Parents are demanding better schools, and they are getting them. You as parents can have a great influence on the quality of educational program your child experiences. People usually get what they really want. They devote their time and resources to those things which they think are most important. If you think that your child's education is important, it will be reflected in your behavior and your demands for the best educational opportunities for your child.

BE POSITIVE

"How to help your child learn" is the central theme of this chapter, as of all previous chapters; a child will achieve much more if the parents are sold on the need for a good education and have a positive, supportive attitude toward schools. Even though you may not consider your child's teacher to be highly effective, you should not be critical in the presence of your child, for if he knows that you have little faith in his teacher's competence, he, too, will have little faith, and this attitude might persist into the future when its reason for being has disappeared. If your attitude is hostile, your child's will be, too, and this hostility and lack of faith will severely limit his achievement. You cannot afford the price of a negative attitude. Sometimes it tears at the heart when you realize the situation your child faces, but you cannot afford to create a wider chasm between child and teacher. Talk with the administrators. Offer ideas, assistance and encouragement both to administrator and to the teacher. Offer support even while you encourage change. Your action will pay dividends.

More often, you will be thrilled with your child's

school, his teachers, and the learning environment. Express this excitement to both your child and his teacher, and offer your assistance in any way needed. But don't become so involved that you neglect your child at home: always be available to assist him in following through with ideas sparked at school, and to help maintain an air of excitement about learning.

PARENTAL EXPECTATIONS

Almost every child is a genius in the eyes of his parents, and failure to achieve at a high level often is believed to be the fault of the school, since few parents will admit that heredity could be at fault. Far too many parents like to gain recognition through their children's achievement, and use their child to this end.

Certainly we want to be proud of our children. We should have high expectations, but it is imperative that parents be realistic and objective about their children. Very few children are able to excel or even perform well in all areas. Just as all boys cannot be major league baseball pitchers, neither can all children be good academic achievers or even be interested in all academic areas. The trite statement that all individuals are different cannot be said too frequently or with too much emphasis. Look at your child as an individual, and acquire the security to let him be himself. Let him help set his goals instead of always setting them for him.

Far too much emphasis is placed on academic achievement and the necessity of a college degree. Only a few years ago there was a vast need for more college-trained people. Today there is a great oversupply of college graduates in many fields. There is a greater demand for people with vocational or technical skills than for college graduates, and in many cases the pay is better also. In the past we have tended to glorify academic achievement and mental accomplishments and to underrate manual skill. This is regrettable. Even those who are endowed with great mental ability do not have the same interests, aptitudes, and goals. Why can't we accept people for their worth as human beings instead of for the degrees they acquire or for the positions they occupy?

If we can't change the expectations and attitudes of the world at least we can be responsible for our own, the ones we convey to our child about himself and school. Check yours: think of ten adjectives right off the cuff to describe the way you feel about your child's entrance into school — or his impending entrance.

12 CHAPTER

It's Up to You

A child's potential for learning is primarily determined by his parents. The inheritance factor transmitted from parent to child is present at birth. The kind and quality of experiences encountered by the child prior to the age of six will determine the extent to which this potential is developed. Preschool experiences have a direct effect upon a child's success in school. The child deprived of experience will have many handicaps to overcome, regardless of his potential at birth.

It is important to remember that early experiences may affect a child physically—blood vessels feeding the brain, and the brain itself, may be enlarged or altered in other ways by early experiences, and your child's learning ability may be enhanced. The school can educate only to the extent that a child is capable of learning, and for this capability, which must be established early in life, you are responsible.

Numerous examples of appropriate preschool activities for enhancing your child's ability to learn have been provided in this book. They were meant only to stimulate your thinking—to get you started—not to provide an inexhaustible list of activities or complete specifications. The intention was to outline the areas in which children need experiences, guidance, and stimulation during the preschool years—the infant with his budding awareness of the senses, the toddler as an explorer, the young child developing in areas of cognitive growth. Activities in visual stimulation, language, number concepts, physical development, grouping and classifying, and self-expression, as well as games for fun, have been suggested as examples of worthwhile experiences for young children.

Whether you take advantage of the suggestions for increasing your child's learning potential is up to you. Will you file the ideas away for use on "a someday" that never comes, or will you really get turned on to those things that are possible for your preschool child, with your help?

Recently I noticed that a child of my acquaintance is not developing in the way that I would have expected. Bright, alert, and eager to explore at age two, he is now, at age four, rather sullen, given to whining, unable to entertain himself, and unresponsive to correction. I know his parents well enough to know that they do not want to rear a child like this at all. They simply do not know how to structure his environment to produce happier results. The problem is not just psychological. The child is not sufficiently challenged intellectually to find satisfaction that makes him feel good about himself. Both parents are educated, courteous, well-meaning adults. They really don't know a better way.

This explanation is certainly an oversimplification of the case but the point is valid. We are missing the boat somewhere if young parents come to this important task with so little preparation for doing the job well. Until a more basic remedy for the situation is effected, it will be the responsibility of parents to seek out what they need to know in order to give their children the experiences they need during the preschool years.

Love is tremendously important—love in all of its important ramifications—enough to provide security, warmth, emotional health; love to provide discipline and limits. But beyond love, you must have an awareness of the possibilities a child has for developing his mind during the early years when he must be stimulated in many areas if he is ever to realize his potential. Failure to receive such stimulation will limit his potential for the rest of his life. This deficiency cannot be removed. For parents who do not have information to motivate them to action, it is regrettable, but for parents who do have such knowledge, it is reason enough to get busy. Within a short time materials will be available to help parents track the intellectual growth of their children. These materials will provide activities like those described in this book, sequenced in such a way that you will be able literally to follow your child's progress as he masters certain concepts and skills. Such tools will be of great assistance, but *you* will still be the key.

The purpose of this book is to impress upon you, as a parent, the extreme importance of the preschool years as a period of active learning for your child. For years educators have recognized the importance of a rich background of experiences for children entering school, but little has been done to encourage parents to take advantage of this critical period in their child's life. This book has provided you with enough information for you to begin. If you haven't already done so, now is the time to start.

Each newborn infant is a unique individual with uncharted potential. Your role is to guide and assist in the maximum development of this potential. The awesome responsibility and the enormous opportunity which are ours were well described by James Agee when he said, "In every child who is born, under no matter what circumstances, and of no matter what parents, the potentiality of the human race is born again." This is your responsibility; how you shape your child's potential is your contribution to humanity. It's up to you.